HOW TO UNMESS YOUR LIFE

AN UNCONVENTIONAL GUIDE TO HEALING, HAPPINESS, AND LIVING YOUR LIFE'S PURPOSE

LIBBY ROBERTSON

HOW TO UNMESS YOUR LIFE

AN UNCONVENTIONAL GUIDE TO
HEALING, HAPPINESS,
AND LIVING YOUR LIFE'S PURPOSE

© Copyright, 2021 Libby Robertson

Published By:

Have It All Publishing
3 St Kilda Road, St Kilda. Victoria 3181, Australia
www.haveitallpublishing.com

First Edition

1 2 3 4 5 6 7 8 9 10

Bulk copies of this book are available from the
Publisher, above, directly at reduced prices.

ISBN: Print version 978-0-6452808-0-7

DEDICATION

For my nieces, nephews, and future generations.

May you never have to 'UnMess Your Life.'
May you always know how amazing and perfect
and worthy you are, exactly as you are.
May you always know how unconditionally loved you are.
May you always know your infinite potential.
May you always know that it is safe to follow your heart and
your wildest dreams, and that you were born to shine.

I love you more than you know.

TABLE OF CONTENTS

PREFACE

This book is intended as an activation.

May each word speak to you with the essence with which it was intended.

May you feel the vibration of each word and allow it to activate the divinity within you.

May you feel, remember, and embody the truth of all that you are.

May you reclaim your freedom and sovereignty.

May you remember the magnificence of all that you are.

So that you can go out into the world.

And shine your light.

In the most YOU way that you can.

You are here, in this life, on this planet, at this time, for an incredible purpose.

You have an abundance of talents, gifts, and abilities ready to be tapped into and brought forth into your life and into the world.

May you walk each day with compassion and kindness and understand true self love.

For it is the shifts we make in our own lives that then allow us to be channels, conduits, and vessels for such deep love and transformation in the world.

May you experience great health, wealth, joy, freedom, love, and prosperity in this life in the fullness of her beauty. Together we heal, together we rise, together we co-create the new Earth.

With so much gratitude for you being here.

I love you,

Libby XO

HOW TO USE THIS BOOK

INSTRUCTIONS ON HOW TO USE THIS BOOK TO ACTUALLY CHANGE YOUR LIFE.

I've written this book for you, with so much love. I hope that by sharing my story and experiences with you, you feel less alone in your own journey. Our healing journeys are so individual and unique, and absolutely not linear whatsoever. No one's journey can ever compare to your own. There is, however, something of a weight lifted off of my own shoulders when I hear others share their experiences and realize that I was never alone in my darkness, nor was I going crazy. It can certainly feel like that. So, I share openly with you, pieces I've often hidden from the world, with the intention that maybe a weight will lift for you, too.

TAKE WHAT RESONATES. Healing, happiness, and living your life's purpose is an ongoing journey, ever evolving, ever expanding, ever changing. I may believe different things than I've written here by the time you are reading this. Please take what resonates with you and leave that which does not. As I said, our journeys are so unique and individual, and this book is intended for you to discover your own truth—who you are, your life's purpose—and pave your own way to happiness. For we can never walk anyone else's path to happiness. Each of us must walk our own.

I am so grateful you are here. I am so looking forward to walking with you throughout the journey of this book and guiding you to explore areas of your own consciousness that you may not have discovered before. Together we heal, together we rise, together we co-create a new Earth. As you read this book, and do the work woven throughout, you may begin to notice changes occurring in your life. Your healing and happiness and this new path of purpose will likely evoke curiosity in those around you. It can be helpful to know that when you begin to walk the path of living your highest purpose, and choosing a life of your greatest happiness, the Universe is always conspiring to support you. This is especially helpful to know when things that are no longer in your best interest start to fall away. Often, when we start our healing journeys, it can feel like things are getting worse! This isn't actually the case, everything's actually getting better… but if things start falling away or changing, please know this is a good thing! Things are shifting and changing and being rebuilt for your highest good. Have faith, and keep going, even if you can't necessarily see results.

Just like planting a new seed, when you water it and give it the nourishment it needs, it will first grow roots, and then grow and blossom above ground. The same is true for us. Sometimes, the roots we are growing require us to strengthen and ground even deeper into ourselves. Sometimes, as we feel like giving up, we're about to burst through the earth into our new chapter (finally!), and the cycle continues as our growth sees us grow, expand, be pruned and shed our leaves, grow deeper roots, expand even more, and eventually, blossom and BLOOM.

PURPOSE PROMPTS: Throughout this book, you'll find **PURPOSE PROMPTS** which are designed for you to get to know yourself better, and to support you in your healing, happiness, and living your life's purpose. These are probably the most important parts of the book if you truly want to change your life. Take the time to answer the questions provided in the PURPOSE PROMPTS and apply the tools and techniques I share with you. This is how you'll actually transform your life; otherwise, this is just another book. If you feel stuck when answering the PURPOSE PROMPTS, simply start writing, even if you think you don't know what to write. Your inner wisdom will begin bringing through insights and awareness, which is what leads to your transformation. This inner wisdom usually comes from your subconscious mind, heart, and soul, which is often difficult to hear or see when trying to think hard about the answers. If you get really stuck, keep reading and put a sticky note on the page, or write down the question in your journal, and come back to it in a few days. This will allow your subconscious to begin working on finding the answer for you, and it may come to you when you least expect it.

SET ASIDE TIME: It can be helpful to set aside time each day, or once a week, or even once a month (depending on how fast you read, and how committed to your life transformation you are). You might like to get up a little earlier, set aside time in the evening, or put 30 minutes in your calendar a few times a week to do the work associated with each chapter.

THE PLAYLIST: I've created a playlist for you to listen to as you do the purpose prompts. You'll find this on Spotify if you search: **'UnMess Your Life playlist'**

SHARE YOUR BREAKTHROUGHS: When you have any breakthroughs or 'aha' moments, please share on your socials and tag me on Instagram **@libbylightleader** or post with the hashtag **#howtounmessyourlife** so I can celebrate with you!

RESOURCES AND COMMUNITY: If at any time you would like more resources, support or like-minded community, visit **www.libbyrobertson.com**

Disclaimer: Libby Robertson is not a medical professional, and everything shared in this book is from her own personal experiences and beliefs. Please seek professional services if you feel the need to talk to a medical or mental health professional at any time.

*Names throughout this book have been changed.

PART ONE: BLACKOUT

BEING YOU

*Like a tree or flower
or mountain.
A mountain doesn't
desire to provide for
the bees;
it knows the flowers
do that.
The flowers don't aim
to provide shade for
animals;
they know trees do
that.
Amplify your radiance
as far and wide as the
Universe sees fit,*

Simply by being you.

HERE I AM

It's one thing knowing you want to change. And another thing actually doing it.

When I started out on my healing journey, I had known for a long time—years, in fact—that I wanted to change... or rather, that I NEEDED to change.

If I wanted to live my best life, that was.

I had always known there was more.

Much more.

And so I began, before I was ready.

Way before I was ready.

My soul was ready all along.

My soul was the one guiding me this whole time. The part of me connected to the Universe.

Ever expansive, loving, and brave.

So brave.

Although, if you know deep down that it's all working out, is that bravery? Or is that faith?

Either way.

Here I am.

Here we are.

Now living the reality I knew deep down was possible.

Receiving messages daily from people sharing how I've inspired them in going sober, or vegetarian, or starting their first business, or discovering their spirituality, or helping them remember their true potential and purpose.

Without me even doing anything. Many of them I have not even had a conversation with before they tell me I have helped change their lives!

And then there is my own coaching and training company that I set up and can run from wherever in the world I choose, where I get to help people change their lives for a living!

And then there are the events and charity functions we host. They're a great deal of fun. I especially loved when we got to deliver money to a local orphanage here in Bali. Seeing the look in those children's eyes reconnected me to a remembering that this work is far greater than us.

And today! I woke up and started my day by giving gratitude for life as I sit in meditation, hearing the birds and smelling the incense burning. Mmmm, the smell of Bali. Living my dream life and helping others do the same. Total bliss.

But it wasn't always this way.

BLACKOUT

I loved to party.

I always had, as long as I can remember.

I had my first taste of beer at four years old, and started my drinking career when I was 13. I remember having booze on the beach over New Year's with my friends on summer vacation.

I spent my teens partying, while still doing really well at school.

I didn't even know I was addicted. I didn't realize that not being able to stop drinking once you'd started was a bad thing. I thought that is just how everyone was. I never noticed it was a problem. Not even when I found myself at the police station after getting into a fight and having my head stomped on by a stiletto (well, by the girl wearing the stiletto), or being taken home by police. I thought this sort of stuff was all normal.

I got good grades. I had lots of friends. I played lots of sports, participated in loads of extra-curricular activities, had a job, and was a prefect in my final year at school.

When I went to university to complete my psychology degree, I thought it was funny when 80% of the lecture theater one day raised their hands when we—first year university students—"technically" identified as being alcoholics.

It was just who we were.

We liked to party.

Didn't everyone?

I didn't even know my habits weren't normal when I would black out and could not remember hours of my nights out... frequently.

18

I thought that was the goal of drinking. It was like a game trying to figure out what had happened, and where my bruises had come from, and where my wallet, money, and dignity had gone?

I didn't even know it wasn't normal when I would have days hungover doused in shame, guilt, and remorse, and wanted to hide from the world for days and eat pizza, never showing my face in public again.

I didn't even know it wasn't normal to binge eat large quantities of food and then throw it up so I wouldn't gain all the calories.

I didn't know it wasn't normal, because it was my normal.

It was my life.

Waking up wondering who I had offended or what I had done wrong.

It was just my reality.

I only began to question the normality of this when it began to impact my work and my relationships. But even then, I didn't think much of it. Arguments and drama had become the normal in my teens and early twenties.

The older I got, and the more I partied, the worse my drinking got. The worse my hangovers got. The worse situations I found myself in. And the louder the gnawing within me became.

The gnawing that was reminding me that this was not my life. I was not on the right path. I had to do something.

In 2015, my best friend and I bought bicycles and cycled the coast of Vietnam during a three-month backpacking trip we took together. Now, she's known me a long time. We grew up together, and many of our teenage escapades we experienced together. Except now, here we were in our mid-twenties, and she reflected back to me that she had grown responsible with her drinking, and I had gotten worse.

One night, I got annoyed at something and took off into the foreign town by myself... with both our passports, putting both our safety in serious jeopardy.

The courageously honest conversation she had with me after that was my biggest wake-up call yet. After that conversation, I began to actively try not to drink. I not only knew deep down that I had a problem, but it was now right in front of me, and I could no longer avoid looking at it.

Every time I went out and tried not to drink, I would become aware of the monster within that screamed for one. Sometimes I resisted, and would celebrate big time; most times I could not.

This went on for months. After I got back to New Zealand, where I was living at the time, my boyfriend was also at the breaking point with me and my drinking.

One day in January, I had gone out around midday to watch cricket with a friend. My phone had died, and my boyfriend was waiting at home for me. When he hadn't heard from me by midnight, he became concerned. 1am, 2am, 3am, 4am rolled around, and he still hadn't heard from me, so he jumped in the car and started driving around the city to find me. The bars were all shutting down and I was walking along the footpath, shoes in hand, wasted.

He was maaaaad. I had started out to go for a couple of drinks in the afternoon, and more than 15 hours later, no news. He thought something bad had happened. I was literally meant to be just down the road. And I was, until my friend and I thought it would be fun to keep partying.

This was the final straw. He had enough and couldn't do this anymore.

I'd heard that phrase plenty of times before.

I hated that I hurt him so much. I hated that my drinking was so out of control. I hated that my drinking was harming yet another relationship.

I vowed to give up drinking.

I was done.

It was a Monday—a new week, a new me, a new life.

Now I could live happily ever after.

When Friday rolled around, it had been a big day and a big week.

"Just one," my co-worker and I agreed when opening the bubbles in the office.

"Just one more," we laughed as we walked to the pub across the road.

"Just one more bar...," as we hopped in a taxi....

Next thing I know, I am in the hospital and a nurse is shining a light in my eyes and asking me questions.

I have a neck brace on, and I can hear people all around me.

I think I just had a full body x-ray.

I try to recall what's happened.

I trace my memory back.

Okay, I was at work, and I had a drink... my god, why do I feel so crappy right now? And then I went to the pub, okay, what next... what happened next? And then I remember a fall.

I remember my neighbor coming to give me a blanket. I was outside; where was I? Oh, I was outside my house? On the concrete, outside. Oh, my head, ouch, wait, is that thick liquid on my head blood? OMG. Am I dead? Am I dying? WTF.

Oh shit. I fell out the window. I remember falling, holy crap, that window is two stories high. Why was I sitting on the window ledge? Was I smoking? Why didn't I just walk outside to smoke?

Where's my boyfriend?

"Nurse, where's my phone?"

No messages.

If I had been at home, surely my boyfriend would know I'm here at the hospital. Where is he?

"Ms. Libby, your parents are on their way."

My parents? Why are they coming?

Confused, I tried to piece together what happened. Where was my boyfriend?

When my parents arrived, and more tests were done, I wasn't allowed to sleep as I had a concussion. I was sobering up and trying to piece together WTF was going on. My Mom shared with me that my boyfriend had called her in the middle of the night and said there'd been an accident. He said I was drunk and had jumped out of the window after we had a fight. The neighbors had called the police. Someone had called an ambulance, and he couldn't deal with this anymore. Turns out I picked another fight with my boyfriend when we had both gotten home from our nights out. He said he was done with our relationship and that in the morning, I was to move out. So instead of going to sleep, I jumped out the window.

Realizing my reality in this moment, I cannot even describe the pain I felt in my heart, my body, and every part of my soul. I had caused this. My actions had created this. My behavior and choices had led me here, to this moment, in this hospital bed, having had yet another relationship fail because of my drinking.

I tried to find anyone and anything to blame, to seek, to take away this pain, and fill this gaping wound in my soul.

I cried and cried, and in that moment, I wished I HAD died.
How was I even alive? Even the nurses and doctors said it was a miracle.

It didn't feel like a fucking miracle.

Not in that moment, not at all.

I didn't want to live this reality. Not this one. Why had I made all those decisions that lead me to this point? I had so many chances and yet I kept choosing the bottle over a great life.

As I was laying there, distraught, seeing the look on my Mom's face as she was witnessing her daughter in so much pain, I had no clue what to even feel or think. A mental health nurse asked me…

"What are you going to do?"

In that moment, with that one question, I felt an energy I can't describe flow through me, and in a split second, I had a bird's eye view of my life and could clearly see my two options:

ME: "I don't know." Or,

MY SOUL: - Yes you fucking do know: "I can never drink again."

And that was it. In that moment, I changed my life.

It was equal parts empowering to speak those words, and the scariest thing I have ever said.

I knew in that moment that even though I had no clue HOW I was going to do it, my entire life had just changed direction.

And since then, one day at a time, my life has become unrecognizable, in the best way possible.

And since then, I have not had a single drink.

Oh, and my boyfriend? After I decided to change my life and moved back in with my parents to start my healing journey, to become the person I knew I was born to be, I sent him flowers to apologize.

Turns out, that same day I'd sent him flowers, he asked the Universe for a sign on whether he should move on or see if we could have another chance.

When he got home from work, the flowers from me were on his doorstep.

Today, we are about to celebrate our second wedding anniversary, and our fifth year sober.

RISE OR FALL

*You can either
rise
through
obstacles
or
fall victim
to your
circumstances.*

A DESIRE FOR CHANGE

In order to truly change your life, and have your own day one. It begins with the awareness of the main thing that needs to change, and your 100% responsibility for changing it.

You don't need to know where you're going. When consciously stepping onto a path of healing and personal betterment, it often comes from a desire of what we DON'T want:

"I don't want to be a wasted asshole any more."

"I don't want to go through any more breakups because of my drinking." "I don't want to be in an abusive relationship." "I don't want to live paycheck to paycheck any more". "I don't want to work in a job that doesn't feel like my life's purpose work."

PURPOSE PROMPTS

What changes do you desire in your life?

_____

_____

_____

_____

What do you want life to look like? To feel like?

_____

_____

_____

_____

What do you NOT want in your life? What do you NOT want life to look and feel like?

_____

_____

_____

_____

What do you want your life to look like, when you're looking back in ten, twenty, or fifty years from now?

_____

_____

_____

_____

RADICAL PERSONAL RESPONSIBILITY

When any area our lives doesn't look like we want it to, it is easy to create excuses or blame your situation, your upbringing, your lack of time or money, your partner, your friend, your cat, the bank, the Universe, your first grade teacher. You get the picture.

The truth is, you and only you, can change your life.

"How can I choose to change this?" is one of the most powerful questions to ask yourself if you're not happy with your current circumstances. Whether it be your income, your job, your living situation, your relationships, your health, your success, whatever it is...comes down to you reclaiming control of your life by consciously choosing to take responsibility for it.

We don't get to choose what life throws at us. But we do get to choose how we respond, and what we do with it.

This one thing alone has helped me in disagreements with my husband, in staying sober, making more money, staying out of arguments, cultivating healthy relationships, and creating the life I now live.

When we allow ourselves to become truly honest with ourselves, especially in the moments we want to tell someone we're right and they're wrong, in the moments when we realize we've fucked up—big or small, when we realize we need to take ownership of our mistakes or place ourselves in the shoes of those around us... we activate a deep level of truth and humility within.

When we're fully honest with ourselves and realize we can't ever control others, we can only control ourselves, our actions, our behaviors, our thoughts, and approach situations from this place, we reclaim our power.

When we reclaim our power, we reclaim our freedom.

When we reclaim our freedom, our happiness is inevitable.

PURPOSE PROMPTS

Think of something specific in your life you want to heal, change or transform. This may be something you've written above, or something else. Be as specific and clear as possible. e.g. I want to stop drinking, or, I want to speak more kindly to myself.

_____

_____

_____

_____

Why do you want to heal, change, or transform this?

_____

_____

_____

_____

What will this change mean for you, for how you live your life? How will this healing, change, or transformation impact your relationships? Your lifestyle?

_____

_____

_____

_____

Now, write all the ways you could implement—or begin to implement— these changes. You may have to get creative here. If it's something that's completely outside your control, instead of changing "it," you may have to employ a mindset, perspective, or attitude shift about it.

_____

_____

_____

_____

What have you learned about yourself in realizing your desire to change, heal, or transform your life?

_____

_____

_____

_____

What are you grateful for about the thing you're changing? (if things have been dire, you may need to get creative here, or instead try asking yourself, "What has this taught me that I can be grateful for?").

_____

_____

_____

_____

What are the consequences—long term and short term—if things don't change and they stay the same?

_____

_____

_____

_____

Now, what are you going to do?

_____

_____

_____

_____

This is your opportunity to make massive change in your life (if not now, when?). It's important to hold yourself accountable to these changes.

Whether you hold yourself accountable through this declaration you've just written, knowing you've been witnessed by the Universe; whether you find an accountability partner online or offline, ask a trusted friend or family member who is supportive of you to hold you to account, or put a post-it note on your fridge—however you do it, ultimately, you are the only one who is able to truly hold yourself to your transformations, healing, and changes.

You've got this.

Strategy to hold yourself accountable:

In order to truly commit to your new path, explore what could potentially be a sabotage for you. Notice your "triggers"—things that evoke a desire to do the thing you're actively trying to change.

In other words, what's usually happening that makes you want to "do" the thing you're trying to change?

As an example, when I made the decision to stop drinking, I listed all the reasons why I might be tempted.

It was an extensive list that included nearly every emotion under the sun that I had ever experienced, along with social events, holidays, vacations, a stressful day, a good day, you name it, it was on that list.

Let's say the thing you want to change is aggression, or reacting with anger. Write out all the things that might evoke anger within you. If it's smoking, or bad spending habits, or biting your nails that you want to change, then write out all the things that usually trigger you to react in this way.

Write out all the 'triggers' where you'll likely be tempted to fall back into old habits.

_____

_____

Now, each time you experience the trigger situation or emotion, what are you going to do instead? By being prepared, you're less likely to fall into past habits, and more likely to achieve what you've set out to do.

_____

_____

_____

_____

This is now your strategy to hold yourself accountable, along with a solid foundation and reasons of WHY it's more important for you to choose the new path than fall back into your old one. And if you ever feel like you might "slip up" in the moment... just remember the consequences of things not changing, and staying the same. The choice is always yours.

A SECRET TO HAPPINESS

The world tries hard enough
To be more,
To feel more,
To experience more,
But they've got it all backwards.

They try to change the world around them,
Even changing their own appearances
To try to feel what they know deep down
Their souls seek,

Searching for what they know
Life can and should feel like.
Rich like dark chocolate,
Free like the ocean breeze,
Content like a rainy autumn day,
Abundant like the lush forest,
Fulfilling like tears of joy.

We have the ability,
Each of us,
To experience what we all seek
And live what we all desire.

The secret is,
All of it comes from within.

Through gratitude, forgiveness, making peace with
the past.

The more we focus on our inner state of being,
Finding our answers within,
Feeling all that we've been avoiding,
And loving all that feels unloved within us.

Day by day,
Our worlds and lives around us
Will mirror and reflect back to us
All the work we've done within.

That is one of the secrets of deep happiness,
And no one can ever take that away!

TRAIN YOUR BRAIN TO BE ON YOUR TEAM

What sort of thoughts are you thinking when you catch your mind wandering, or when you first wake up in the morning?

Train your brain to be on your team. When you first wake up in the morning, practice finding something to be grateful for. I used to wake up in such a grumpy mood almost every single day. I began to realize this was getting in the way of my happiness, so I decided to begin practicing gratitude before I got out of bed in the morning. Sometimes, I would be so stubborn in my grumpiness that I would struggle to find gratitude for anything; it felt so far out of reach. Day by day, literally one day at a time, I would practice. If I couldn't find anything, I would try again the next day, or even come back to it a few hours later that same day.

One of my clients, Toni, had a similar issue. From the outside, she was successful. She had a large social media following. She travelled, had her own business, and was on track to hit her goals. But she was depressed. When I was going through a gratitude exercise with her, we realised she struggled with this, too.

We were sitting in a café together and I asked her instead, "Well, have you ever had a moment where you looked around at your life, paused, and just thought "OMG, this is AWESOME?"

She looked at me curiously, looked away, sipped her matcha latte, and took a big breath as she thought about it. She looked back at me, and I noticed a shift in her energy, "Yeah, I have."

"Good," I replied. "Can you feel that same feeling when you think about it now?"

"Yeah."

"Great. There's your starting point."

Perhaps like Toni and I, you also have trouble "finding gratitude." Instead, see if you can find a moment in your life where you've looked around and thought "OMG, this is AWESOME." Maybe it was at a concert. Maybe it was when you achieved a goal you had set for yourself. Maybe it was on vacation, or spending time with friends. Whatever it is for you, feel that same FEELING in your body. Notice where in your body it is. As you breathe in, double that feeling. As you breathe out, notice the feeling expand in your whole body.

Now, begin to practice that.
Practice starting each day by tapping into that same feeling.
Practice ending each day by breathing into this same feeling.

When you find your mind wandering throughout the day, practice this "OMG this is AWESOME" feeling.

This is how you begin training your energy and emotions to let more happiness into your life. Most people wait until they experience things or situations to "make them" happy. The truth is, happiness is an inside job. It's up to you to learn to cultivate this feeling, perhaps even before you see any reason for it in your outside world. Don't wait for situations, things, or people to "make you" happy. You'll struggle to find true happiness if you're always waiting for the world to give it to you. Train yourself to allow gratitude and happiness to flow through you regardless of what your environment and world around you looks like. Then no one can ever take it away.

There will come a time when you're ready to begin saying "thank you" for life, and for the world around you, and actually mean it. Gratitude will become your natural state. But first, it starts within.
Try this every day for at least 30 days. Track your energy and emotions and notice the shifts beginning to take place.

PURPOSE PROMPTS

Write out five things in your life that you're grateful for:

1.
_____

_____

2.
_____

_____

3.
_____

_____

4.
_____

_____

5.
_____

_____

Observe what feeling is evoked when you think about these things. How can you now enhance or evoke that feeling in more areas of your life? It may require training yourself to get into this energy. You might like to journal, meditate, or simply find something to be grateful for, first thing in your day.

OBSERVER VS. DETECTIVE

As we go through big changes in life, it's so easy to try to figure out WHY everything is happening.

Why time feels different.
Why the colors and the world look different.
Why the stuff that used to matter no longer bothers us.
Why surface conversations feel dull.
Why we're facing challenges.

Why shopping malls feel overwhelming and riddled with toxic consumerism.

In order to shift into your next level with greater ease, it requires a new level of observation of the shifts, and seeing things for what they are rather than what they mean.

BEING AN OBSERVER

When we look at things for what they are, we allow ourselves to sit in our heart space and allow everything to unfold naturally and with flow. We maintain our center and power and vibrate at a frequency that allows our inner and outer world to remain in balance and harmony. We're open to the lessons being brought to us, and because of that, open to the blessings and manifestations that come.

BEING A DETECTIVE

If we try to find reason, meaning, and cognitive understanding in why everything is happening, or we attach an idea to whether it's good, bad, ugly, necessary, not right, too much, not enough, too painful, too easy, too frustrating, not in our plan, or too far out of our control, and try to place meaning onto things, we often get our emotions and minds involved. This, then, interrupts the natural flow of the universal workings happening around us and within us, and prevents the very things we've been desiring to come into our lives from actually coming in.

Blessings, miracles, and abundance are often on the other side of contrast, challenges, or growth-provoking situations. Every cloud has a silver lining. Always. And you don't need to understand why the cloud is grey or made up of water particles to know there is a silver lining. The sooner you surrender to the cloud, the sooner you'll learn what the silver lining is.

When you're going through shifts, allow yourself to be an observer and let everything simply be, rather than trying to figure out why or getting your emotions involved.

If it is unpleasant and uncomfortable, simply observe that it is unpleasant and uncomfortable.

Be present with it. Don't fight it. It will pass.

If you decide that being in this state of unpleasantness and discomfort is bad, then you add resistance to the natural happenings of growth and expansion.

Let it be.
Observe it as you grow through it.
It's happening for you.
It's a sign of your up-level and releasing all that's not serving you.
You're rising into your authentic self.
Into higher alignment with your true self.
A body of light, a being of love.
There's nothing to fear.
Nothing to figure out.

Open your heart, and you'll be guided to everything you require, everything that is of assistance to you being of highest service in the world and across the universe.

Life is much easier when we allow things to be what they are, from a place of observation. This might also require deeper faith that any darkness is going to be over soon.
This too shall pass.

It's all perfectly imperfect; it's all divine.

Let it be. It is what it is. Watch your manifestations come to life with greater ease, greater flow, and in greater abundance.

PURPOSE PROMPTS

Sit in stillness for a moment and take a big nourishing breath. Sigh out any stagnant energy (this helps clear the minds noise to hear the wisdom of your heart). Then, answer the following questions:

What feelings have you been judging yourself for, or trying to avoid, suppress, or numb?

_____

_____

_____

_____

Why do you believe that is?

_____

_____

_____

_____

What would happen if you let the feelings be there, without judging, avoiding, suppressing, or numbing them?

_____

_____

_____

_____

THE DIVINE DESTRUCTION

Destroy
Destruction
To Destruct
To Re-Construct

Destroy the toxins that poison your life.
Destroy all beliefs that no longer serve you.
Destroy all stories you have been carrying that do not belong to you.
Destroy the fears that hold you back.
Destroy the drama your ego is attached to.

Create so much Destruction in your life that you must rebuild it.
The Destruction will literally shatter your reality and you'll slowly see
the infinite possibilities of ways to rebuild.

The beautiful thing about total Destruction is that it allows us an
opportunity to build a brand spanking new, solid Foundation.

The beautiful thing about building a brand new Foundation is that we
can create it however we see fit.

You see darling:

When we Destroy all that no longer serves us, just as a town that has
been devastated in an earthquake, we get to redesign our lives for
our highest good, our greatest potential.

Just as a council would redesign the devastated town for the highest
good of its townspeople, using the natural landscape to its greatest
potential, we get to do the same with our lives.

Of course, when you can see an opportunity to rebuild, it's much
better to do so than to wait for an earthquake to force a rebuild.

The same goes for our lives.

For me, it took total Destruction: a magnitude ten earthquake in my life for me to totally rebuild.

My town, -my life- is unrecognizable today compared to before the absolute Destruction. Of course, I would not wish Destruction that strong upon anyone. I would recommend everyone strengthen and rebuild as soon they see an opportunity to do so.

That is: **You do not have to wait for your world to crumble before you rebuild.**

What can you start removing, Destroying, and rebuilding right now, today, to start Creating the most incredible, strong, solid life for your greatest potential, and with impeccable Foundations?

QUANTUM ABUNDANCE

From here, you'll receive insights into my Quantum Abundance Method to begin magnetizing your dream life and discovering your purpose.

When we talk about manifesting and creating your dream life, we often forget an important piece of the puzzle. We talk about going from point A to point B, and forget about an important layer in between A and B.

If creating your dream life was as easy as thinking about it and becoming that person, many of us would be much farther along in our growth journeys and living our dream lives already.

When working with clients, I guide them through my Quantum Abundance Method, a five-part process, to get from A to B.

The QAM recognizes there are three layers of abundance.
The first is *where you are now*.

The third is *where you want to be.*

Wait, what about the second?

The second is *all the subconscious beliefs you hold in your body-system that require healing, releasing, unhooking from, to be a vibrational match for the third layer.*

People will often achieve their goal (going from A to B... or from layer 1 to layer 3)... and then bounce back to where they began.

Why is this?

Because they haven't become a solid container and energetic match to be able to maintain or hold what they've just received.

This is why a large percentage of people who win the lottery end up broke after a few years. Or when people come into large sums of money and end up losing it, giving it away, or having nothing to show a few years later. Or people who lose weight and put it all back on again.

It was also the reason why for many years before I actually gave up drinking, I would do short stints sober, but could never last much longer than 10 days (I think 10 weeks was the longest stint I ever managed since I was 14).

If our deep rooted subconscious beliefs are constantly telling us we're not worthy, not enough, we're going to be rejected or judged, we can't out-shine those around us, or something bad is going to happen, we don't deserve that, someone is going to take it all away, it won't last, I'm a bad person, I can't get it right, it's too much, I can't do this, it's just not who I am, if I have this then someone else is missing out, what will everyone around me think, it can't be this easy...

We're going to reject anything from our lives that doesn't align with THOSE beliefs.

Just like someone having an organ transplant: if their body doesn't agree with the new organ, the body rejects it.
The same explains our energy field and body-system.

Mind-body, physical-body, emotional-body, energy body.

Yes, even the good stuff. Even the dreams, the goals, the amazingness.

And if we do not energetically reject it, it will feel like a struggle to keep it. The fears will keep coming to the surface—fears of losing it, everything disappearing, failing, everything going back to how it was.

Whenever we're in fear, we're not in love.

When the fears come into your awareness, it is an invitation to teach your belief system that it's safe. That you are worthy of magnificence. That you were born being enough. That you are loveable. That you are love. You are a good person. You are allowed to live your dreams.

So, our job is to not only attract our desires, but keep them, and continue growing and evolving with more and more ease as the journey goes on. Our job is to unhook from the belief-structures energetically repelling all that is not in the same frequency.

Where do our beliefs come from?

Before we're born in this life, we are a soul.

On a soul level, we've had lifetimes before this current life we're now living. We choose our parents and our families based on what we will learn in that specific human experience, for the evolution of our souls. Remember, growth and evolution come from contrast, challenges, and conflict. This can be a hard one to digest, I know. This is why it is often said our families are our greatest catalyst for growth. Whenever I am working with clients who have estranged from their families, we go through a process to learn and embody the lessons learned, regardless of the difficulty and painful experiences, for their own path, growth, and evolution.

We carry information in our souls from past lives.

This information is stored in our body-systems as an energetic belief in our field. This information holds a vibration contributing to our holistic belief system. The vibration we hold determines what we magnetize, or not, into our life.

When we are born as human beings in this life, our genetic make-up also holds information passed down from our ancestors. We carry information in our bodies from seven generations before us. The belief patterns you live your life with have been wildly influenced by those who walked this planet before you in your family line.

From the time of conception in our mother's wombs, we are beginning to be influenced in our beliefs. The soul is already present, and the human baby is being formed. We begin to become influenced through not just what our mothers consume physically through food, but energetically and emotionally. Just as research has shown the benefits of playing music to your unborn baby in utero, the baby is also impacted by emotions and experiences the mother has throughout pregnancy.

From birth, we begin developing our response to the world. We use our brain to compute everything we are absorbing, seeing, witnessing, and hearing through our senses, and these sensory experiences begin forming pathways in the brain, called neurological pathways. When a sensory experience happens over and over, it creates a stronger pathway in the brain and will eventually create an imprint so strong we have no trouble recalling information. You can quite easily go outside and recall what a tree is. You can see moving objects with limbs and recall that these are people. You can probably ride a bike or drive a car without thinking about it. You've had these repeated so many times that recalling the information required to interpret your world and surroundings feels effortless.

However, the things we don't use so much, or that we don't need to navigate the world, are all stored in our subconscious mind. Every conversation, everything you witnessed, every experience you've ever had... good or bad.

From birth to age 12, the brain is forming its perception of how to navigate this world, and your life, at rapid rates. It's like a sponge, experiencing so many things for the very first time.

As we get older and our cognition develops, the brain begins to absorb external information not as "new," but instead, it recalls the piece of information it already holds within to process and interpret.

Eckhart Tolle talks about being in the "now" and seeing everything as new, to truly see it for what it is, not what our past experience of something has been and thinking, therefore, this must be the same. He talks about going outside and seeing a tree. Most of us just look at a tree as just another tree. But if you take time to become present and in the now, you'll notice the shades of colors, the shapes of the leaves, the texture of the branches, really beginning to see the tree for the first time, even if it's been in front of you for years.

See how this begins to play out in other areas of your life.

If, when you were younger, you witnessed your Mom enter relationships and her boyfriends would leave, and then you saw her emotional experience afterwards, you might approach your own relationships with a belief or fear that your own partner will leave.

Or, if you witnessed your parents arguing about money, your beliefs around money might be those of hardship or arguments, and now you might see money as something to fear or avoid or as being responsible for hardship.

Perhaps you experienced being bullied at school or your friends ran away from you, so you might now have a fear of friends leaving, of not fitting in, or find it difficult making friends now.

Or, if your parents constantly told you they loved you, they were proud of you, and that you were amazing and talented, you might have incredible self-esteem and confidence as you navigate the world now in your adult life.

How you see the world now is massively determined by the subconscious and unconscious beliefs you hold within about how to navigate the world, and that have largely been absorbed during your first twelve years on this planet in this life.

Now remember what we said about personal responsibility right at the start of this book?

You didn't get to choose the experiences that happened to you or around you.

But your healing is your responsibility.

Unlearning non-serving beliefs is your responsibility.

Learning to love yourself, even if you do not know what that looks like, and haven't experienced it from anyone around you before, is your responsibility.

You can either use your experiences as excuses or opportunities. If you grew up in poverty or experienced the sort of trauma you would not wish upon anyone, you now get the opportunity to not only heal it for yourself, and to let your pain teach you about your own magnificence and deeper purpose on the planet, but you also get to learn how to love yourself in the process. It is my hope that we can then use our healing and transformation to support others in their journeys as well, creating a ripple effect of healing around the world.

On a soul level, many healers and people here to help humanity heal and rise, have been born into family lines with deep pain and suffering. We have endured experiences we would never wish upon another person.

Because you have the strength to heal it, you have the strength to rise because of it. Our pain doesn't need to break us. It gets to become our power. Our gift. Our strength.

Regardless of what you've experienced. If you are here right now reading this, you have an incredible purpose. You have an incredible role to play in helping humanity heal. In helping to end suffering and experiencing love. To be a better world for future generations.

You have that power. You have that ability.

You might not know what it looks like, or how, why, or any of the details. And you don't have to.

The more you focus on healing yourself, unhooking from past beliefs and learning to love what seems like even the most unlovable... you not only do so for yourself. But you do so for the entire planet.

Thank you for your healing. Thank you for your rising.

It might not be easy, and it certainly won't be linear, but on the other side of transmuting pain and darkness into love, is the most incredible freedom, bliss, joy, and state of abundance.

At your core, you are love. You are literally a fragment of Source, God, The Universe, Creator, Great Spirit. You are here getting to know yourself through the power of contrast. And when you realize you are not your pains, or your experiences, or stories, or family, or even your name, you are the awareness of it all... you unlock the layer of depth from within that allows you to be a channel for such incredible impact and change on the planet, and to experience all this life has to offer.

By you healing and learning how to love all of you, through every moment of now, determining what you choose to believe about yourself, about your life, about your future, about your ability and worthiness to achieve your goals and dreams, and to say "Yes" to your greatest and most magnificent life, you positively impact humanity and the planet forever.

You can't learn how to truly love and forgive and release and embody the best version of you that you know how, and NOT leave a positive impact on the planet and the lives around you.

When you have faith knowing you are a being of love, that the Universe is always supporting you and guiding you, even when it doesn't feel like it, you have the courage to dive deep into your holistic body system. To unhook from the information you're subconsciously living by, and the frequency of all beliefs that are determining what your external world looks like. You have the ability to achieve incredible results and outcomes in your life, in an illogical amount of time.

PURPOSE PROMPTS

HOW TO USE THE QUANTUM ABUNDANCE METHOD

Step one: Get honest with yourself

Get clear on level one. This is where you are now. You simply have to observe your life currently to see where you are. Remember, regardless of where you are in life, you have the power to change how things are. Wherever you are now, that does not determine how able you are to make huge changes in all areas of your life. How willing you are, does.

For example... I'm doing okay in my life, I have a home to live in and a family who loves me, but I know deep down there's so much more I can be experiencing. I haven't yet started the business I know I want to begin, even though I don't even know what the business is just yet.

_____

_____

_____

_____

Step two: Visualize with your heart

Place your hand on your heart. Take a big breath in. Relax. Don't rush this step. You're tapping into the wisdom of your heart and soul here.

Let your heart guide you as you answer the following:

Where do you truly want to be in life? What sort of person do you want to become? What do you want your lifestyle to feel like? What do you want your relationships to feel like? What do you want to spend each day doing? What sort of income do you want to generate? What do you want your health to look like? Your spirituality? Your wealth? Your happiness?

Write this out as if it's already happened. Remember, it doesn't matter where you are now. Anything is possible if you allow it to be so. Be as detailed as possible.

For example... I am someone who others completely trust and respect. I wake up every day and choose what I get to do each day. I have plenty of money to do the things I want to do. I have incredible relationships with my family and a close inner circle of friends. I have a successful business, helping people all around the world. I am truly living my life's purpose. I feel grateful I'm living in the world at this time, where I can work from anywhere there's internet, and have the freedom to choose how I live. I am connected to The Universe and meditate every day. I am always guided and feel so supported by The Universe. I am so grateful I made the decision to pursue this path, even before it made sense, and stayed on this path even when it felt like I was going nowhere.

_____

_____

_____

_____

_____

_____

_____

_____

_____

_____

_____

_____

_____

_____

_____

_____

_____

_____

_____

_____

Step three: Shine light on the shadows

Knowing that you are not your fears, and that you have the power to change your beliefs, look right at the very things you may have been trying to avoid, or which have been the reason for you to procrastinate or delay taking action on your desires and "goals." Look for any beliefs that may be acting as "blocks." This is like placing a cosmic magnifying glass over the limitations you have internalized so that you can see them, and then choosing whether to believe them, or whether to leap into the unknown and begin to take action by re-writing these limitations with new, empowering beliefs.

What do you truly believe about where you're going, what you visualized, and what you desire? What fears or doubts are there? What limitations or current circumstances feel like they are blocking you? What is it that might be making you feel "stuck" on how you can achieve your desires?

For example... I feel like I don't have the confidence to start a business. I'm afraid I'll fail or that everyone will make fun of me. I don't know how. I've never done anything like this before. No one in my family has ever done anything like this before. It feels too hard or like it will take too long. I feel too young / too old.

_____

_____

_____

_____

_____

_____

_____

Step four: Rewrite all non-serving beliefs

Remember you have the power to choose what you believe. You are not your beliefs or your fears or your limitations, and you can choose to re-write anything that is not helpful to where you are going. This is where the work is, as most of us believe our thoughts to be true.

After observing the thoughts and beliefs you uncovered in step three, what do you now choose to believe about yourself? What do you now choose to believe about what is possible for you?

For example... I choose to believe I will find the confidence to start a business. I choose to believe that failure is not an option, and I can only ever learn. I choose to be open to the possibility that things may work out even better than I could have expected. I choose to love and accept myself and follow my own heart.

Whatever other people think is only their opinion, but at the end of the day, I am the one living my life. I choose to be courageous and brave enough to go first, to try things no one else I know has done. I believe I will be shown the way, even if I don't know just yet. I am in charge of the decisions I make. I choose to start now; it's better now than never. If not now, when? I choose to believe I am a good person. I am worthy of an amazing life. I choose to believe I am always supported and guided by The Universe.

Step five: Take imperfect action

Often, we wait until everything is "perfect," or until we have all the answers laid out in front of us, but that hardly ever works. Instead, it may leave us waiting forever, and never actually doing what we desire to do. Whatever you can do now, do it. Sometimes you have to take the first step, then the stairs will appear. It's never going to be perfect or feel like you thought it would when you begin, and there will be a million reasons (excuses) as to why you should wait, but remember, you get to decide what thoughts to listen to, and if there are none that are actually helping you get to where you're going, then choose new thoughts that will.

What would this new version of you now do to get closer to Step Two? How would they think and act and make decisions and talk to themselves? If you put yourself in their shoes, what would be the first thing they did to begin getting from where you are currently to where they are now? Be creative here and keep writing until you hear your own solution. Remember, all of your answers are within you.

For example... Start an Instagram account for your business idea. Have the conversation you've been avoiding for years. Begin writing the book starting with a short blog. Write a letter to your past self. Attend the retreat or hire the mentor. Google how to start a podcast (and start one).

_____

_____

_____

_____

_____

_____

_____

_____

WHO DOES SHE THINK SHE IS?

She is so powerful.
She speaks her message, her truth, loud and clear,
And with unwavering faith.

She is decisive.
She has confidence in going after what she wants.
She is making a wild difference in the world.
Just who does she think she is?

She leads the way and goes first.
She nourishes her body with the best food.
She moves her body each day with love.
She is sexy and fun and wild and free and adventurous and courageous
And spontaneous and outrageously loving. A huge heart for her people
And this planet and humanity.

She blames no one and takes full responsibility for her actions.
She always learns from her mistakes.
She doesn't need permission or validation from anyone.

Her faith is unshakeable.

Who does she think she is?
She leads with her heart and thinks with love.

I don't get it; who does she think she is?

I AM SHE
SHE IS ME
WE ARE HER
SHE IS US

We expand with confidence.
We grow with clarity.
We consciously love.
She is her wildest, boldest dreams.
I am my wildest, boldest dreams.
We are our wildest, boldest dreams. I am becoming the
best version of me that I can absolutely possibly be.
This is what I desire, this is what I choose. And so she
decided: now is the time. And as simply as that, she did.
And she is: whoever she desires to be!

PURPOSE PROMPTS

Visualize your future self. The version of you who is living the reality you tapped into while you were going through the Quantum Abundance Method. Connect with their essence, what they believe in, what they stand for, how they choose to take responsibility for their life and their happiness, how they choose to live.

Just like the above piece, "Who Does She Think She Is?" write out your own description of your future self, unique to you.

_____

_____

_____

_____

_____

_____

_____

_____

_____

Be sure to take a photo or make a copy of what you've written to connect with your future self often. No matter how "close" you feel to the version of you that you've just written out, please know—it's already a facet of you, and that transformation happens one day at a time.

HAPPINESS FIRST

Still blown away by
The magic of life,
For a second chance at life,
And for this human
Experience.

All the
Hard decisions
And continued action
Without even seeing "the results"
Have been one hundred and
Eleven percent worth it.

Focus on your
Happiness
And mental + spiritual + emotional
Health
First.
The external results
Will come
After.

PART TWO: SLIDING DOORS

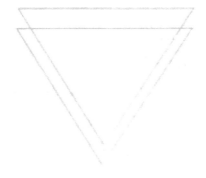

LEAPING INTO THE UNKNOWN

How often do you begin something and quit only a short while later? Your New Year's resolutions? How are they going? It is easy to stay committed when it is easy. When it is hard, then the real work starts.

When we decide to change our lives, there's gotta be a pretty compelling reason to do it. How many dreams and desires have you seen fall away, only because you couldn't follow through or make the necessary changes to bring them to life?

Most people think that change is something that you "do."

We look at what changes have to be made in our environments, relationships, lifestyles—all things outside of us. We give our power to external circumstances and wait for something to fall into our laps, or to make the necessary changes for us.

Change is an inner game.

If you are going to change your entire life, you will also have to change your entire way of "being." Your mindset, emotions, energy, and physical body are all going to shift.

The reason most people never reach their dreams or change their lives to become the people they know deep down that they have the potential of being, is not anything to do with external circumstances. It's just that they begin to try and take action on things from the same perspective, viewpoint, and mindset they've always had.

Your new life is going to require a new outlook.

That being said, it is important to activate a part of you that knows WHY you're changing your mindset, outlook, attitude, and perspective, as well as the external life changes, habits, and outcomes you desire.

The multiple times I tried to give up drinking before I finally did, I approached each situation as the same version of me I had always been: The Party Girl.

When the only identity I knew was "The Party Girl," it took all my willpower NOT to drink.

On the 30th of January, 2016, I had to find a new way to approach my life if I was going to be successful in my new pursuit. I also had to know why.

In the past, I didn't have a compelling enough reason to truly commit to my desired change. I didn't have enough motivation to follow through with the half-assed decisions I made to "never drink again."

This time was going to be different.

Not just because I'd lost the man I thought I was going to marry, and *another* relationship because of my drinking.

But I knew deep down that if I did not change... I would die.

That, for me, was a compelling enough reason to find a new approach to my life.

Instead of identifying myself as The Party Girl, I began to identify myself as "Being Sober."

This is easy to type into one sentence here, but this change came from days where I would wake up feeling broken and confused, trying to plead with the Universe to get my old life back. I didn't know anyone who didn't drink, and I'd partied my entire life.

Shedding the only identity that I'd ever known was one of the most painful experiences of my life. But in those moments of darkness, I KNEW I had to find a way. And I did.

I knew I had to think differently and do life differently if I wanted different results. So I began meditating, journaling, and listening to podcasts and exercising and channeling all the energy I would have used on drinking and hangovers into bettering myself.

I remember, on the weekends in my new life, my body was used to only having 4-6 hours' sleep from years of partying, so if I'd had an early night on a Friday (a whole new situation to find myself in), I would wake up at 3 or 4am. I used this time to go to the gym and focus on my physical health.

I learned how to be alone with my mind and learned about inner child healing. I learned how to love myself, even when it felt impossible to do so. It is only through hindsight I learned that when you learn how to love yourself, from the inside out, your entire life changes.

The drama ceases, the negative thought patterns subside, the self-loathing dissipates.

And day by day, by learning how to stay on this path you have chosen, by tapping deep within to find WHY you are doing this in the first place, that evokes a deep emotion from within; you begin to create spiritual resilience in the moments your mind tries to take you back into your old way of being.

In one of my most challenging days a few months into my sobriety journey, I was meant to be getting ready to go away for the weekend with some girlfriends (girlfriends who respected my sobriety), but this would be the first time the four of us would be together since I had stopped drinking. And instead of packing my bags, I found myself knocked to my knees with grief—grieving the death of the version of me I could never be again and feeling the pain of not knowing who I was. And there I was, curled up in a ball on the floor having a breakdown instead. Feeling the pit of helplessness, my entire mind screamed at me to just go and get a bottle of wine (or twelve), and this pain would all go away.

And in that moment, I felt my soul's strength kick in and override the noise of my mind.

I asked the Universe for help; I asked Dane to message my girlfriends and let them know I wouldn't be coming. I knew I needed to simply focus on myself right now. I consciously decided I would get through this moment and day without drinking, and I continued my breakdown. Multi-tasking at its finest. This was also the moment I began to learn that breakdowns are what lead to breakthroughs.

I was so connected to my "why" that failing just wasn't an option.

If you want to change anything in your life, you've got to have a deep, penetrating reason why, if you truly want to succeed at it.

And this isn't just related to healing addictions. This is the same when I face obstacles and challenges in my business, relationships, and other areas of my life.

In order to get to where we're going, we have to become emotionally connected to why we are doing something in the first place, and ask ourselves how we can take responsibility, be open to new solutions, or find another perspective.

When we can be okay with changing the constructs of our minds and current limitations and be open to new ways of thinking, acting, and showing up in the world, for ourselves and those around us, we let our hearts and souls guide us and open to a whole new world.

Oh, and on that. Become okay with the unknown.

Your autopilot daily life and habits are from the accumulation of your memories and experiences. You've got a subconscious learned response about how to navigate this world. These make up your ego... the construct of your identity formed by the mind.

When you begin learning how to love fully, you are living deeper from the heart. This also allows you to restore deeper belief and confidence in yourself and open a deeper ability to trust those around you, yourself, and the Universe.

When you begin making changes in your life, your ego (who lives from past constructs stored in your entire body-system) will try to hold onto to the past. It's safe that way.

When you begin to choose your best life, it means making different choices and more often than not, opting for the unknown, as scary as it is.

Safe and comfortable is choosing the path where we know the outcome. It's familiar. It's easy... until the discomfort of staying there gets too loud.

Living in this unknown—which I believe is the path of the heart—and creating a new way of being is a daily commitment to getting to know yourself, dating yourself, and having trust that EVERYTHING is working out for you. The challenges, obstacles, the things we feel are working against us... have been given to us for us to grow. We either see them as obstacles, OR what I prefer to call "growth provoking opportunities."

Whenever you're faced with a challenge, like leaping into the unknown, see if you can find the energy of excitement or curiosity about what growth this is going to bring.

Then, of course, learn and apply the lessons.

PURPOSE PROMPTS

What's an obstacle you're currently facing or have faced recently?

_____

_____

_____

_____

How does it make you feel?

_____

_____

_____

_____

When was the first time you remember that same feeling?

_____

_____

_____

_____

As an adult, you get to choose what is true for you and what's not. What do you wish to lovingly tell the version of you who first experienced this feeling?

_____

_____

_____

Now, with this current or recent obstacle, what lessons are you choosing to learn if you were standing in the shoes of your future self?

_____

_____

_____

_____

It is natural for us to remember things that went wrong, or when things didn't work out. Our systems are wired that way. To make massive change in your life, you're going to have to become okay with the unknown. Teach your system to become okay with the unknown, or at least find proof that on the other side of change, you're going to be okay.

Think back to one or two times in your life where you made a decision purely based on faith, where you leapt into the unknown, and things turned out fine, or if you're lucky, better than fine.

_____

_____

_____

_____

Moving forward, whenever it comes to leaping into the unknown, use these memories to remind yourself that you're going to be okay (in fact, more than okay, The Universe is always working in your favor).

FORK IN THE ROAD MOMENTS

There comes several times throughout life when we see the fork in the road of our journey, and which path each may follow based on the outcome of one decision.

Life is filled with these mini forks daily.

Sliding Doors.

The Butterfly Effect.

When the big ones—big choices and decisions—approach, we often hesitate. Many avoid choosing so as to not choose the "wrong" one.

There is no wrong one.

You cannot get it wrong.

Your life is made of the adventures that come from fork in the road decisions.

If it comes to it, and the decision does not lead down the path you thought it would, create a bridge to the other path. Change course. Change direction. Make a new choice.

As we go through life, we will often see two or more very different paths we could go down.

I remember many pivotal points in my journey when I decided on one rather than another.

Were they scary? Most times, yes.
Did it mean committing to one and ruling out the other? In this particular case, no.

This is a life of faith, following love and joy, knowing that waiting to see both outcomes isn't an option, and the only option is to make a decision or to forever stay in the limbo of indecision.

When I finished my Bachelor's Degree in Psychology at university, I always thought I'd go back and complete my Master's or a Doctorate and become a registered psychologist.

I spent nearly a decade exploring both myself and the world, waiting for life to show me the right path, while simultaneously doing my best to follow my heart.

I had an opportunity to go back to University and complete what I thought I would. And instead, I chose the other path.

The less "safe" one.

The one that might mean I'm judged by my peers or receive more sideways glances than the other socially acceptable and professionally understood path of the psychologist.

Instead, I chose to follow my soul's calling to Shamanic training.

Consciously choosing to take the road less travelled. At least in our current Western world.

I know that, perhaps like you, part of my soul's purpose is to help normalize spirituality in the modern world. To help bridge the gap between ancient and new. To help end modern suffering such as the mental-health epidemic, rising suicide and addiction, anxiety, and depression. To show humanity, through my own experiences and work, how powerful we are, and more importantly, that we are far beyond the mind-body construct that much of the Western world is built upon.

We're absolutely doing better as a collective. Spiritual and emotional well-being is now being understood. But you and I—we've got work to do! Until humanity is free from suffering, there is much healing to be done. We're an entire collective; when one of us heals from our own suffering, we will each be guided in our own unique ways to help others. And so, whatever it is you're guided to do, when it comes to your healing journey, follow that. You will never know who else it will be able to help down the road. There's no right or wrong. Your life, your path, your alignment, your healing, your personal journey. No one can tell you how to feel, what to think, or what decisions to make, even when it might appear that they can, and do.

We always have choices, to listen to our heads or our hearts. Our beliefs or others'.

Whatever you choose is up to you.

And remember, it's at the fork in the road moments that our greatest adventures begin.

WHAT'S YOUR OTHER REALITY!?

One night, as we sat down together for the evening, Dane and I spoke about another reality that could have been us. One where we made more "sensible" decisions.

A reality where, that time in our heated discussion sitting in the car one day, talking about investing $6,000 to pay for my first coach, we chose to keep the money in "savings" instead.

One where, instead of trusting my soul and leaving corporate management, we opted to stick it out and suppress the pain because #whataboutthemortgage.

One where we said "no," as most people probably do, instead of opting for the illogical "yes."

... over and over and over again.

One where instead of donating my car to the mechanic when I started my business and using that money to pay for a business course, I did the sensible thing and kept my car and paid for it to be fixed.

We both saw the path that would have been much EASIER. Probably much "safer," more "realistic," and more "logical."

The times when leaping was the scariest moment of our lives and we asked, "Fuck, what if it doesn't work? What if we lose everything? What if we fail?"

"How do we know it's going to work? Where's the proof?"

And like that first coach reminded me,

We chose to listen to the whispers of our souls:

69

"What if it's better than you could imagine?"

"What if you gain more than you could know?"

"Your belief is all the proof you need."

"Faith is HOW you know."

And as we looked around at our reality, our lives, our relationship, our beautiful environment, our incredible businesses, the people we've helped, the families we've impacted, the communities we've supported...

We were both about in tears at realizing what "could have been" had we chosen logic and reason instead of soul and faith.

Your divine guidance will rarely make sense.

You have been blessed with a vision for a reason.

However, it is up to you to have faith.
No one can make the scary decisions for you.
All of your answers are within.

And as you leap, fly, and co-create with the universe, miracles and magic become a way of life.

SURRENDER

There comes a time in our journey that requires us to surrender. **I surrender.**

It becomes a conscious choice to let go of the beliefs, the patterns, the only identities we ever knew, the perceptions of the world we thought were 100% true, the traumas we inherited: **we heal.**

This path is not linear. There is no one right way. No one size fits all. It's messy. It's powerful. It's glorious. All at the same time.

I dig deep and go beyond my current human existence.
I consciously choose to be a conduit for my divine mission.
I see my ego mirrored back to me in the bumps along my journey.
I commit to this work in serving this planet.

There are moments of surrender that define our path.

Mind or heart?
Logic or faith?
"This is all I know" or "I have no idea what this is about to look like, but it just feels right."

The deeper I go, the more I discover we live in this world fuelled by ego. I look back at some of my goals, even a week ago, and painfully see the ego basis of those goals. I see where I've put my worth and success in numbers that hold no substance.

My soul came here to do so much, and I realize the places I was placing importance on things, my soul doesn't care about. When I'm confronted with ego and gaps of my highest alignment, old patterns want to come in and shame me and blame me.

It is in these moments I choose to accept it, forgive it, shift it, and change it.

As my heart cracks open with my cosmic remembering and I connect with divine love, I'm reminded of all the incredible possibilities in front of me, if I continue to choose love.

A life committed to love and faith continues to invite inner inquiry to let go of the fear.

To share from our hearts, regardless of what others might think.

Have faith.
Surrender.

It will help someone else to feel less alone in their journey.

I choose to surrender.

I choose to break rules and speak of things that might shock some.

This path is one of courage, but with this amount of faith, I am never alone.

PURPOSE PROMPTS

What is something you have always wanted to do, but have been too afraid to?

_____

_____

_____

_____

Why do you feel you have been afraid of this?

_____

_____

_____

_____

Instead of being afraid of it not working out, or making the wrong decision, or failing, or losing everything, you asked yourself instead: what if it worked out better than you could ever imagine? What would be the benefits? What would it feel like to succeed?

_____

_____

_____

_____

CONTROL

We never really have control of the things that happen to us in life.

We can attract and manifest more positive experiences and design a beautiful life through our thoughts, yes absolutely. But life will always throw unexpected obstacles our way.

It's in these moments we grow the most.

When we let go of controlling everything in our lives and start focusing on controlling HOW WE RESPOND, life goes much, MUCH smoother. We are the only people responsible for our attitudes. We have 100% control of our attitudes. No one chooses our attitude but us.

We can literally CREATE a more enjoyable life by choosing CONTROL of our RESPONSES and REACTIONS and LETTING GO of trying to control the SITUATION. This is also how we create our "destiny" or "dharma."

We don't get to control what happens to us, but we do get to choose how we respond. And it's in our response that we create our realities.

I began writing this book nearly three years before it will actually end up being published. I had spent many days upon days writing, many words that will never be read by another soul. Many tears were shed as I typed experiences that I'd never shared before out onto the pages. I finished the first draft just over a year ago and posted a celebratory #YAY on my Facebook page to mark the moment.

A few days later, I was making some changes to my business systems and needed to set up some new software; my husband, Dane, offered to help. My MacBook requested a system update, so he accepted it and the laptop updated itself, as it promised.

When I opened the draft a few days later to begin making edits, nothing was there.

Turns out something happened in the system update, and the entire book had been wiped out.

I didn't know whether to laugh or cry.

When it comes to situations over which we have no control, we have a choice:

1. To complain at the lack of control, the situation you've found yourself in, or the way someone's done something to you—i.e., throw a tantrum, lose our shit, blame others, and become a victim.

Or

2. Change the situation to a more positive one simply by changing your attitude and perspective on the situation you're in—i.e. pause and take a breath or walk away to calm yourself down, then look for the gifts of what this may mean; trust things are happening for the better (even if you don't know why just yet), and take responsibility for what you can do about it.

Because you DO have control over your response.

It's up to you.

If you find yourself reacting and unconsciously choosing option one, forgive yourself, and then come into option two. The more you practice this, the more you'll naturally begin to respond from a place of empowerment, embodied in the knowledge that you create your reality by the way you choose to respond to the world, and your life will positively begin to reflect that.

Had the book situation happened a few years earlier in my journey, I would have sat bitterly and resentfully in option one for weeks, months, or maybe even years.

But it didn't happen years earlier. It happened exactly when it did.

And because of years of consciously practicing this, my response to the situation, over which I had no control looked something like this:

Me: OMFG. What? Omg. What? What? Where's the book?!

Me: *feeling rage boiling inside me* "Dane—what did you do to my computer the other day?!"

Dane: "I set up the system thing and did the update for you."

Me: *still feeling rage boiling* "My book's gone; why did you do the system update?!"

Dane: "Your laptop needed the update. Those update notifications were popping up, so I did it for you."

A bit of a (one-sided) heated conversation (the heated one being me) took place as I tried to take control over the situation and bargain for control by trying to find something / someone to blame.

I took myself into the upstairs bedroom to breathe and come back into my center. I laughed as I realized the lost book was not the book I was meant to write, it was purely for my own healing, and that the Universe had another plan in store for me. I chose to believe there was a greater unfolding taking place and that I would simply have to write a new book and trust that this was all happening for the highest good for all. And here you are now reading this. I hope you're enjoying it so far! I hope you're noticing things already beginning to change for you and that this book is adding value to your life.

I went downstairs, apologized to Dane for trying to blame him, and shared my new excitement about what this situation now meant!

So, I started again, and trusted things were working out better than I could even imagine.

And had that book not been wiped out, you would not be here reading this book now.

PURPOSE PROMPTS

What situations have you found turned around by choosing your attitude instead? How did it work out for you? How did you feel after choosing the more empowering response?

_____

_____

_____

_____

_____

What's a situation you're currently experiencing (or have recently experienced) that you can't control? How would your future self choose to respond?

_____

_____

_____

_____

_____

Can you think of a situation, if you're being honest with yourself, that you would handle differently now? Don't beat yourself up—this journey is about learning, not judging. It's through learning from reflection that we gain insight to be able to make positive change moving forward.

_____

_____

_____

_____

DO THINGS TODAY YOUR FUTURE SELF WILL THANK YOU FOR

Doing something for the first time is often what prevents us from doing it at all. Whatever the "big" future thing is, hold it at the forefront of your awareness each and every day.

Make choices and decisions that will bring the vision closer to you.

You are only going to get better at whatever it is you are afraid of starting.

You don't need fancy systems or gadgets or anything else you're trying to tell yourself you need in order to begin. Just begin. Take action. Ideas are just ideas until you follow them on through. And don't we all have amazing ideas?!

When you start before you might feel ready, and keep going when you still don't feel ready, the vision you hold will become more touchable than you know. Your heart's whispers, your soul's desires, the deep knowing in the pit of your stomach. The "is it even possible?" kind of feeling.

They're all things guiding you, steering you in the direction of the place where your future self is hanging out, saying "thank you" for the decisions you made that led us to this moment.

And that is an incredible moment.

THE POWER OF INTENTION

Whenever I'm working with clients, whether it be in their money goals, or impact, or projects, or whatever it is they are calling about, I ask them, "What is your intention?"

It might even be something small, like doing a livestream, or slightly larger, such as having a conversation with someone who has the power to make big changes in the community. Either way, I always guide them to embody their deeper intention.

Here's the thing.

When your intentions are matched with your desires, you become a magnet for what it is that you want.

However, if your intention isn't matched or isn't even aligned with your desire or what you say you want, the distortion in your energy field creates a distortion in your level of magnetism.

The goal is to ensure that your intentions, and the deeper intention behind the intention, are aligned with what you say you want (even to the Universe).

One of my clients once said to me, "There's no hiding on this journey, is there?!"

Nope.

If you say your desire is to impact one million people's lives, but your intention is to live a small life, yet provide abundantly for your family, there is a mismatch between the outer-desire and the inner-intention.

Neither is right or wrong. The goal is to make them match.

It requires a huge level of self-honesty.

What do you actually want? What do you desire?

What's your intention BEHIND the desire?

The intention is the grounding, the foundation, that anchors the desire.

When you let your inner intention guide you, you'll be able to find the alignment within.

PURPOSE PROMPTS

Sometimes our deeper intentions and true values can be drowned out by the sound of our current reality, or ego-based desires (desires shaped by the outside world rather than the truth of our heart and soul). A solution to this can be connecting with our future, in hindsight.

Imagine you're about to turn 100 and your loved ones are organizing a birthday party for you. Close your eyes and visualize yourself at your 100th birthday party.

Who is around you? What are you celebrating most about life? What is important to you? What do you prioritize? How have you lived your life that you are most grateful for? What isn't important? What have you let go of? What do you no longer prioritize or give thought to? What type of person are you? If a loved one gave a speech here, at your 100th birthday party, what would they be saying about you?

_____

_____

_____

_____

_____

_____

_____

_____

_____

_____

_____

_____

From here, what do you now see that you value the most?

_____

_____

_____

_____

These are the foundations for your personal values—the values that stem from your deepest inner-most intentions. How different or similar are these to what you believed your values and intentions for life were? What changes now get to take place?

_____

_____

_____

_____

_____

_____

Now write down your top 3 - 7 values for life.

Whenever you are making decisions or choosing the direction to take things in your life, refer back to your values and ask yourself if your desires match. This will support you in ensuring your desires and intentions match, a potent combination to activate a certain magnetism as you reclaim power over your life and create the future you actually desire.

A DECLARATION

To make the biggest impact on the planet, in humanity, in our lives, we must look at our intentions and declarations. Most of us go through our days through habit. When you come back to daily intentions and daily declarations, you give yourself the gift of clarity, grace, and flow.

From here, you'll begin to step into your highest potential by stating exactly what you are choosing. From here, decision-making and getting clear on your direction become a much easier co-creation among you, your soul, and the Universe.

I am on a mission of the Universe. A devotion and commitment to love. "God is my oath", this is what my birth name, Elizabeth, means.

I declare to always stand in and honor my truth, regardless of surroundings and situations.

I declare that I will fully integrate and embody all the upgrades and downloads as they synergize from heaven to earth so I can support others to do the same.

I choose to heal through self-discovery, and the ancient teachings of shamanism. I choose to be the embodiment of my message. To speak words of high vibration and truth.

I choose to be in ceremony, ritual, and commune with the Universe, Great Spirit, Ancestors, Mother Earth, and all of her beings—forests, plants, oceans, mountains, and animals—both physically and in spirit.

I choose to be love. I am the embodiment and expression of all I came here to be and experience at this point in time.

I am guided by trust, faith, and intuition, my NO and YES clear and strong, loud and clear.

I am whole. I am free.

I honor my truth, my divine light, and I choose to be a conduit for the Universe to bring through what it desires. I release the grips of my ego and choose to play large. I choose to radiate light and follow my heart, releasing the need to please others and following my highest truth and path. I forgive all, including myself, whom I am still harboring pain towards. I transmute this into light, love.

I choose fun, play, and deep gratitude.

This is my declaration. This is my intention.

AND SO IT IS.

A WORK IN PROGRESS

Beautiful soul, this is always a work in progress.

If you were to set an intention, a declaration for your life, what would your heart pour onto paper?

What would be expressed if you went into meditation, connected with your soul, and let your expression pour out? Would it be journaled via words? Would it come out as a song? Perhaps you'll be called to dance your declaration, carving movements of energy to be carried by the winds to the all-knowing-all-seeing-all-hearing Universe. Perhaps you'll paint or draw or simply sit and FEEL.

Your declaration, your intention, can never be right or wrong. It is as you are willing to experience life, to express your soul, to embody your mission, through your natural desires and gifts and talents and joys.

If you gave yourself permission to re-write how you have to "do" life, what would you do? How would you be? How would you create and express yourself?

There are no rules.

You create your own.

This is how you unlock your highest path and your ultimate declaration.

PURPOSE PROMPTS

Sit in stillness. Perhaps create a beautiful space for yourself with candles and incense and music, or outside sitting in nature, and bring your attention to your heart. Feel a ball of energy, love, and gratitude begin to wash over you and through you, coming from your own heart center. Invite your soul— your higher consciousness, angels, beings of the highest light, God, Source, Creator, Great Spirit, The

Universe, unconditional love, whoever you feel connected with the most—and through your mind's voice or out loud, ask it to support you in embodying your truest, highest self, as you write a letter of declaration for your life.

There's no right or wrong way to do this. Let your heart and soul guide you as you write, and enjoy.

_____

_____

_____

_____

_____

_____

_____

_____

_____

_____

_____

_____

_____

_____

_____

_____

_____

PART THREE: SPIRITUAL REBELS

WHEN YOUR FRIENDS AND FAMILY DON'T GET IT

You, beautiful soul, are here on one of the greatest journeys you could be on. The journey to your greatest life, your greatest self, your greatest experience of this life, and all that it brings.

Which is also probably one of the most rebellious things you could do in this world.

To set on your own path, away from society's normal, and choose you.

You have a magnificence within you waiting to be expressed and experienced. You, and you alone, are responsible for all choices you make. No one can coax you into anything. Ultimately, it is you who says yes or no. (And how blessed are we to be living in a time and society where this IS the case for so many? It's my vision for all of humanity to have this level of freedom.)

And you, beautiful soul, have an incredible life waiting to be lived when you give yourself permission to let go of social constructs and the beliefs of your family, friends, career, industry, and community.

You are in control of your destiny.

You can't choose what happens to you, but you can choose your response. This is how you turn fate into destiny. This is how you live your highest path. By choosing to take ownership of your decisions and break free from the mould placed upon you by the noise of the world around you.

You, beautiful soul, are here to make a wildly magnificent impact on humanity. Your healing, your choice to take your highest path, impacts everyone around you.

We carry energetic information in our bodies and DNA from our ancestors. The experiences of those who walked this planet before us are carried in our energetic makeup, and impact how we view, see, and respond to the world. When you are on your own self-love and healing journey, you are simultaneously healing your ancestral line and any future generations.

I remember one time in my journey, I was feeling blocked when it came to stepping into new levels of leadership and receiving my next level of income, so I decided to go and "explore" what it was. I realized that I had a core fear around responsibility that was energetically blocking me from stepping into my next level.

I couldn't work out where it had come from; I had no logical reason to fear responsibility. In my conscious mind, I felt ready, so I knew there was something I couldn't access with my conscious mind. I did a healing session on myself and realized that it wasn't my fear.

It was a fear from my grandfather's mother.

Yup. Wild, I know.

In my session, I was shown my grandfather as a little boy, and his mother taking care of many children in the time of the Great Depression. They didn't have any money, and a memory popped in my mind from when I was a child and my grandad would tell me stories of how his Mom used to sew clothes for him and his siblings from old potato sacks. They didn't have enough money for shoes, so when they were walking to school in the cold New Zealand weather, they would stand in cow-patties to warm their feet up.

Now, in my session, I could see his mother and feel HER energy and stress at having to provide for her children without any money.

With tears streaming down my cheeks and a deep honor and respect for my great grandmother (whom I'd never met), I used my techniques to shift this energy and fear from my own body-system and replace it with love. For myself, and for my ancestral line.

Where there is fear, there is not love.

When we are healing, we get to transmute all the fear in our bodies into trust, acceptance, and other frequencies of love.

After that, I went on to receive several incredible opportunities for my brand, and to have my biggest week in sales in my business.

Trust yourself.

If you want more from life, to feel happier, healthier, wealthier, sexier, whatever it is you desire... it's because whatever you desire is meant for you. If you continue to live your life on others' terms, you might experience a good life, but the KNOWLEDGE you have that there's more will never go away—not until you choose to trust your heart, make decisions in faith, and leap into the unknown.

When I had to make scary decisions to change my life, I taught my brain how to trust more.

When I left my ex-fiancé in my early twenties, my logical mind said to stay, and my heart said it knew there was a better life and partner out there for me.

Our lives were so intertwined: we met when we were both living in London and we moved to Australia together. We experienced so much together and planned our entire futures. We were going to move to Brazil and help in orphanages there. We were going to get married and start a family. We loved each other deeply.

But it wasn't a healthy relationship. I knew I had to leave.

I could clearly see the path where we stayed together: Mind.

I couldn't see the path at ALL if I were to leave: Heart.

Neither option was easy. I knew leaving would be hard. But I knew staying wouldn't be easy either.

I remember thinking back to other times I had been in similar positions and had to make similar decisions... I never had to leave a man I was engaged to before, but surely I experienced something similar...

Had I?

A few years before that, I packed up my life in New Zealand and booked a one-way ticket to London. It was my first time overseas. I didn't even have a passport before that, and I moved to the other side of the world.

I had to leave my whole life in New Zealand behind—family, friends, everything I'd ever known.

I had chosen to leap into the unknown.

And it was better than I could ever have expected—that leap into the unknown.

Okay, so surely this would be the same then? If I could be okay with a massive decision into the unknown THEN, surely, I could do it NOW...

So, I did.

It was my birthday. I didn't want my new year around the sun filled with any of the things it had been in the past. I went home on my lunch break—I was working as a travel agent at the time—and packed my bags. I said goodbye to the "exotic" life where we were due to fly out to Brazil and left... realizing I also said goodbye to the toxic life I had been enabling.

It was the best decision. But I only learned that in hindsight. Sure, it was painful. But the pain of staying would have been suffocating.

Since then, whenever I'm faced with decisions like those, I ALWAYS opt for my heart, my soul, THE UNKNOWN. The illogical. The "it-doesn't-make-sense-on-paper-but-it's-a-feeling-that's-hard-to-explain" kind of decisions.

Why?

Because I now have a library of information in my body-system that when we LEAP, it's going to be okay; we are going to be okay. It may be uncomfortable at first, but the rewards and freedom on the other side of the discomfort are phenomenal and more often than not, better than I could EVER have imagined.

The same is available for everyone.

When you KNOW the desire and magnificence buried within you is waiting to be expressed and experienced, you then KNOW when you make leaps of faith from the calling of your heart, you are aligning to that very desire and magnificence.

We fear the unknown.

When we can learn to embrace it, our greatest life awaits.

Take the leap. It's infinitely worth it, whatever the mind might suggest.

Had I listened to ANYONE around me at any of these times I was making decisions based in faith, there is NO WAY I would be living the life I am today. Especially when almost everyone (except a few special people who are the only ones still in my life) around me was questioning my sobriety and wondering.... when I would have a drink with them again.

A few weeks into my journey, I was with some friends at a wine and food event (I didn't know any other way to socialize at that stage; my whole life had revolved around booze, so when I got sober, I just tried to fit my new self into my old life), I was on about my 4th Red Bull when a friend said, "Come on Libby, just have one wine with us, we won't tell anyone."

"Na, I'm good, thanks."

"Come on, one won't hurt."

"Um, yes, it will, I'm not drinking. Now let's go dance"

No one, not a soul, could feel what I felt when it came to this level of commitment to my new life-path.

When I tried to explain myself, some sort of got it, but most didn't. I stopped trying to explain myself when I realized no one else knew what I did about me, my soul, and my life.

This level of self-permission to fully accept myself literally comes from the depth of my soul. Radical self-acceptance is the foundation for standing strong in your new path.

People will ask questions and potentially judge. However, it's not your responsibility to convince them of your new life, and their judgments are simply reflecting back a part of themselves they've not yet met or understood.

I can't even tell you how many people who judged me wildly years ago have since reached out and thanked me for the positive impact I've had on their lives since.

It's not your responsibility to explain your life to anyone. It is your responsibility to take ownership of your life and live it.
Wildly, rebelliously, authentically to who you are, and who you came here in this world to be.

And remember, when choosing your most magnificent life, those who are meant to stay, will.

PURPOSE PROMPTS

If you had no fear of judgment or rejection from your loved ones, what would be different in your life? What would you be doing, or no longer doing? Who would you become, or no longer be, just because that is what is expected?

_____

_____

_____

_____

_____

What is required to make a small (or big) change to be truer to yourself, and who you were designed to be?

_____

_____

_____

_____

What courageous conversations may need to be had?

_____

_____

_____

_____

_____

What may be the consequence of having these conversations?

_____

_____

_____

_____

What would be the long-term consequences if you didn't have these conversations or make these changes?

_____

_____

_____

_____

Now, what are you going to do?

_____

_____

_____

_____

LIFE IS A CEREMONY

Everything is a ceremony.

From the food we eat to the conversations we have, to our commune with nature.

Each new day, each sunrise and sunset, each time we make love, each time we gaze into someone's eyes and see their heart, their soul.

Our ancestors remind us how sacred life is, and when we learn their teachings, we remember the very celebration of life.

Start each day with "Thank you."

If there is one secret strategy you're looking for to change your life, it is this,

"Thank you."

Speak words of increase.

Speak words of love.

Speak words of contribution.

Let nature teach you about your truth.

Be strong like the oak tree.

Be fluid like water.

Let go like the wind.

The more connected to your heart, to nature, to your rhythms and cycles you are, the more flexible you become. From here, from a place of being with what is, remembering the ceremony of life herself, the more you will accomplish.

Ceremony is a way of life here in Bali.

I will never forget being at a fire ceremony where I sat with a Balinese Priestess.

Each day, she gets up at 4.30am, showers, meditates for an hour by herself, then holds a fire ceremony to give gratitude to the gods, ancestors, guardians of the land, parents, friends, all things in life, and asks forgiveness for wrongdoings and blessings for her loved ones... all done through chant, mantra, offering, prayer, meditation, and intent.

I've been practicing meditation and my own spiritual practices for nearly a decade now, and to be honest, I feel like I'm still a beginner.

When people ask me to teach them things, I feel like, "Who am I to teach you?"

And then I remember—we are all just doing our best to walk ourselves, and each other, home.

Knowing this is my life's work and soul's mission, I continue to study, practice, and delve deeper into my spirituality, my desire to be the full embodiment of all that I came here to be.

Tapping deeper into my gifts and bringing forth as much light as possible into the world, my only job is to do this for myself. The deeper I go, the more light I hold, the more I can guide others to their light, their truth.

As one of my teachers says, never trust anyone who tries to get in between you and your connection to the Divine.

TURN YOUR LIFE INTO A CEREMONY

Start each day with an intention for the day ahead.

Consciously give thanks for things silently as you move throughout each day.

Create a positive morning routine.

Bless your food each time you eat, giving gratitude for all the land and hands involved to get the food onto your plate.

Take meditation or mindfulness breaks every few hours. Connect to your breath, slow down throughout the day to breathe and feel the life each breath gives you.

Walk barefoot in nature at each opportunity you get. Place your feet in the grass often. Create opportunities to get into nature more.

Move and nourish your body in new ways that bring you into a deeper relationship with this beautiful human body you live in.

Journal, meditate, or pray daily.

Tell people you love them, express your gratitude and appreciation of them.

There's no right or wrong way to turn your life into a ceremony.

When you can consciously choose your thoughts, your actions, your choices, and your habits, and begin to celebrate being here on this planet, having this human experience, you will open a depth within as you begin to remember what it feels like to live a life of deep fulfilment.

GOOD THINGS TAKE TIME: UNDERSTANDING THE MYTH

Yes, but no.

Good things take alignment.

Time isn't linear as we always thought it to be.

It is simply a change in moments of now.

Think about this.

Time is simply a change in moments of "now."

You can keep going through life, day after day, and not do ANY work on yourself. You can remain the same, and you might get places. It will most likely take a while.

You can also meditate and use positive affirmations and make positive changes in your life. That might speed things up, but it will likely still take a while. OR, you can decide what you want, who you want to become, and begin showing up every day as THAT person.

On the flip side (and this is how I began), you can decide who you DON'T want to be, and change everything that's keeping you stuck in that loop.

For me, I didn't WANT to be a wild party girl, battling shame, anxiety, depression, bulimia, guilt, and never-ending hangovers for the rest of my life. I didn't want to have to spend every Sunday apologizing to whomever I'd upset the night before. I didn't want to keep checking my bank balance and see transaction after transaction after transaction showing me all the clubs I had been to, and all the rounds of tequila I had bought for strangers.

I didn't WANT people to look at me like, "I know what you did last night," and argue with myself about whether I should ask them what it was or not.

I didn't WANT to have all my lovers leave me because I prioritized parties and prosecco over them.

None of that was who I was, who I knew DEEP DOWN that I came here to be.

So, one day at a time, I chose to take one step forward, even when I didn't know if my other foot would follow me, let alone which people in my life would come with me as I embarked on this new journey.

I had no idea where I was going.

But I sure as heaven wasn't going back to the hell I had just come from.

Now, I place a hand on my heart each day, and tap into the FEELING of what I want life to feel like.

I look around me at all the beautiful things to be grateful for.

I feel my feet on the earth and take time to feel centered and grounded in simply being here, on this planet, as a human being.

I used to want to escape so badly. Now, I don't want to leave. I love this planet, and I want nothing more than to give each day the opportunity to fully experience all that life has to offer.

The beautiful thing about being human is that we can create and change and adapt so easily. If we don't like something, we can change it. If we want to create something, we give thanks for it coming to us and know that we are fully supported.

If any part of us doesn't believe our dreams are really possible, we look at that dis-belief and ask, "why not?". Often times, we realize that we're carrying beliefs that aren't ours (we might have picked them up from society, our parents, TV and media, school, our experiences.)

We were born expansive—knowing and believing that everything is possible.

That doesn't change. We just begin wearing layers of external beliefs as we grow up.

To truly create what you desire is not a matter of time; it is a matter of your courage to face your entire self, especially the unpleasantries you might have experienced, and forgive them, have compassion for them, release the beliefs associated with them, and create new aligned beliefs.

Here's where we're flipping the paradigm on what most people tell you about manifesting.

Because most people try to ignore the unpleasantries.

It's human. We try to avoid pain.

But it's not helpful if we truly desire to live our greatest, happiest lives.

I know that is super contrary to what you're probably expecting. "Focus on the positive, look at what you're grateful for, count your blessings, be the light." But here's the thing, if we ignore what's really under the surface, then we're trying to build a castle on sand, without digging below the surface to create those super solid foundations.

Whenever I work with clients who are stuck in their personal growth, I always go to the root beliefs of what they're carrying. And while they have been meditating and using positive affirmations to try and reach their goals, and on the surface, they're doing everything "right," when we dig deeper, we realize that they experienced trauma as a child and their body-system is still carrying that trauma response as the core belief.

So, what do we do? We look at the core beliefs creating a self-sabotaging loop. We release the emotions, we do inner child and energy healings, we re-wire the energetic belief system, and align on a vibrational level to the very person they want to become, in alignment with their highest self. I'll share a technique you can use for this in a moment.

This is what alignment is—the Full Body Belief System that matches up mentally, physically, energetically, and emotionally with your desired goals.

Mis-alignment (and why "good things take time") is often an uphill struggle to achieve goals, because while mentally and physically you might agree with your goals, energetically and emotionally, you don't.

When you want to Quantum Leap your life, or achieve your goals quickly, it's not a matter of working harder, longer, or with more blood, sweat, and tears (although depending on your goal, that can also come into play). It's about asking, "Who do I get to become? How does the version of me who's ALREADY EXPERIENCING THAT show up?"

And most importantly, what fears, doubts, or dis-beliefs are currently stopping me from FULL-BODY-BELIEVING that my goals are already done?

Then, shift them, re-write them, become best friends with forgiveness and compassion, and feel the physical shifts in your body as you literally release all that is not in alignment with your goals, creating new belief systems and structures in your entire holistic being.

This new level of quantum time means addressing the things we're taught to ignore.

It means facing the things you are not proud of.

It means apologizing for your wrong doings (where appropriate).

It means accepting what is and making peace with the past.

From this place only, you are able to create a solid foundation to receive your soul's desires.

You can only grow as deep as you dig.

These alignment strategies will see you surpassing all logical time when it comes to achieving your goals.

This is because you are working with the depths of your soul, that knows no time or space, and only knows how to magnetize your desires when your full-body-belief-system matches the energetic frequency of those desires.

PURPOSE PROMPTS

FULL BODY BELIEF SYSTEM HEALING AND ALIGNMENT TECHNIQUE

1. THE ORIGIN

Discover the sabotaging loop.
What is the pattern you keep observing in your reality?

_____

_____

_____

When did this first begin? (It may involve different people, different situations, or different environments, but the FEELINGS of the pattern are the same or very, very similar. It may even be something you observed others doing while growing up).

_____

_____

_____

_____

_____

_____

What beliefs are driving this pattern?

_____

_____

_____

_____

_____

2. THE LESSON

Release any emotions that want to be felt or expressed. Often, these have been trapped for years, or since the original time of the pattern coming into play, and many times after that. In order to break the pattern and release the deep emotions and beliefs driving the pattern, we must learn the lesson we are being taught. The lessons are usually driving us to more love, truth, sovereignty, and free will over the lives we are choosing to live and the beliefs we are allowing ourselves to live by. What lessons are you learning, and choosing to learn, through the origin and beliefs that have been driving this pattern?

_____

_____

_____

_____

_____

3. THE ALIGNMENT

This is where you get to re-write all the beliefs that are outdated and not conducive, supportive, or helpful for where you're going, the life you are consciously creating, and the person you are becoming. This is where you literally get to change the trajectory of years, decades, lifetimes, or even generations of patterns and cycles.

As you are going through this, also notice the removal of the past emotion or feeling, and what the new beliefs FEEL like. This is how you will re-write your full body system to be in alignment with where you're going, mentally, emotionally, energetically, and physically.

What are the new beliefs you are calibrating to, that are in full alignment with the person you are becoming and the life you are creating?

_____

_____

_____

_____

_____

_____

FINDING YOUR RHYTHM

When you give yourself permission to unhook from society's constructs of how we're taught to hustle, grind, and live in a linear Monday through Friday, 8 - 5 world, everything changes.

Everything in this world follows seasons, cycles, and rhythms, including our bodies.

If you begin to tune into your body's natural rhythms, you'll begin to notice the cycles and seasons of your mood and energy, and find ways to work smarter, not harder, in every area of your life.

I used to feel stressed without even knowing it. If a door would slam, or I encountered a conflict, my fight / flight / freeze survival instincts would kick in and I would easily fright or run from situations (or if it were an online "hater," I would freeze). One time, I was dealing with a crazy challenging situation that really threw me, and I spent days in bed, so afraid to show up online or in my business at all.

Understanding that much of it was trauma-related, I realized that even while healing, there was an undertone of stress in everything I did.

I intuitively knew that in order to take my life to new levels, I would have to learn to become fully grounded and centered in myself to be able to stand strong in challenges and not let external events impact my ability to love and live fully.

When I began studying Shamanism, I realized I had been trying to live my whole life in Summer. I was always on the go, and would wait until I burned myself out before properly resting.

Female bodies have a built-in monthly season indicator. Many people are affected by the moon's cycles, whether consciously or not. Many people notice seasonal energy cycles, even experiencing seasonal depression. When we begin to tap into our natural rhythms and to track our moods; energy; thought patterns; desires; mental, physical, and emotional patterns; and observe, without judging, simply becoming aware of what's going on in our holistic body system; we're able to find our flow much more easily.

Everyone has their own unique rhythm, and the more you listen to and trust your own energy and patterns and cycles and rhythms, the easier it will be to find, honor, and master living in your unique state of flow.

Obviously, we still need to function in the world, and our world, so it's never going to be one hundred percent perfect. However, when you're aware of your natural cycles, it is much easier to plan, prepare, and live in your highest alignment.

For example, when I realized that I was always trying to live in "summer," and would literally be forced into "winter" (through illness or burnout), I began to track my natural monthly cycles, seasonal patterns, and even annual rhythms. Then, I began to include my own autumns, winters, and springs, meaning that I hardly ever get sick, never reach burnout now, experience more balanced emotions (waaaay less mood swings and yo-yo energy), deeper happiness, contentment, and bliss. And even when it sometimes feels like I'm working "less," I'm way more productive and have way more fun.

I also introduced this more around the time I made a commitment to eliminate complaining from my vocabulary and mindset, so some of this may be related to that as well. Either way, life, love, and business just feels way easier and more joyful.

Each month, each of my seasons lasts about a week. We also experience each season in our daily rhythm, as well as our annual rhythm.

WHAT THE SEASONS MAY LOOK LIKE IN YOUR DAILY LIFE:

AUTUMN

General: this is a time for creating simplicity, preparing for winter, tying up loose ends and errands, tidying or clearing out your physical space, beginning to slow down, setting up additional support systems—for example, hiring help around the house or with your kids—setting you up for as much space as possible in "winter."

Daily: night time, before sleep. Introducing an evening routine can support you in reflecting on the day, letting go of all that no longer serves you, reflecting on any challenges and finding learnings, forgiveness, and gratitude practices to support your personal growth, so that tomorrow, you wake up a stronger, more evolved version of you.

Monthly and Annually: preparing for an energetic "hibernation," of sorts. You may be doing reflections on the year you've just had, noting any key learnings and lessons. Reflecting on the things you're especially proud of or grateful for. Anything you'd like to release or let go of. If you're running a business, you may be setting up more systems and automation or outsourcing or delegating to give you more space during "winter" for you to go within as deeply as possible to strengthen your leadership and company vision and impact.

It's also often a time to appreciate the harvest of the season's seeds you've sown. Or an opportunity to reflect and choose whether or not you'd like to plant those seeds again or choose new seeds.

Perhaps your inner-seasons follow the monthly moon cycles. In this case, this may be when the moon is waning.

WINTER

General: this is a time of shedding, rejuvenating, going within. This is often when our inner strengthening takes place —learning and integrating lessons, preparing for the next cycle, a time of rest and introspection. When a woman is on her period, this is considered her own personal winter. It's an important time to go within, with a clear (as much as possible) schedule, to focus on the wisdom and guidance that comes during this phase, and that can only be truly accessed when we switch from the "busy-ness" of Western life to the stillness required for a wholesome and balanced inner-world and psyche.

If you're naturally introverted, you'll likely feel most at home in this season of your cycle.

Daily: sleeping—set an intention before sleep of anything you would like to heal, or you would like answers or insights. Anything that you would like to let go of, forgive, or learn lessons around. Each day is an opportunity to start again and leave the day we've just had in the past.

Monthly and Annually: more time inwards. Generally, in the Earth's winter, the days are shorter and colder. This can be a great time to let go of any projects or commitments not actually in alignment with your values and desires. More time journaling or meditating or simply "being." You may feel a desire to curl up with a book next to the fire and release all guilt of not "doing" (and may even find you can actually achieve more). This is totally rebelling against the Western constructs of life, but it is an essential part of growth and evolution. Honor your inner rhythm here.

Monthly, this may be when there is a new moon.

SPRING

General: this is a time of planting seeds, setting intentions, starting projects, planning, acting on new ideas, cultivating relationships, brainstorming inspired insights that may have come through in your winter phase.

Daily: morning, upon rising. This is a great time to "plant seeds" for the day ahead. What energy do you want to cultivate? What mindset do you choose to have to set yourself up for an empowered day? Finding something to be grateful for first thing when you wake up is a great place to begin, as is energy work like reiki or tai chi, meditation, journaling, or setting intentions for your day ahead.

Monthly and Annually: you're coming out of an inner hibernation, perhaps feeling a bit raw and tender from all of the "shedding" that took place, in your life or in your identity. An opportunity for rebirth is here. Cast visions and vibrations of the new cycle you desire to experience. Where you've been, what you've experienced, or who you have or have not been, is no limitation to what you can create and what type of person you can choose to become. This is a great time to set goals and implement new plans for the cycle ahead.

Monthly, this may be when the moon is waxing.

SUMMER

General: this is a time of abundance, more projects on the go, heightened energy. Socializing, launching new products or businesses, hosting events, you may even notice a superpower, feeling invincible and like you can effortlessly juggle many things at this time in all areas of your life—business, career, family, and community. This is natural, don't beat yourself up when it feels more challenging in your inwards seasons. This is what systems and building a support network are for. Unfortunately, society only acknowledges this phase, which might explain many things in the world. It is taking people like you and me and countless others to begin making changes around this, starting with ourselves.

If you're naturally extroverted, you'll likely feel most at home in this season of your cycle.

Daily: the main day time. Mid-morning to evening. You'll generally have more things to do, as life calls you each day. Within each day, regardless of what the outside world demands of you, see if you can still show up, in harmony with your own flow.

Monthly and Annually: longer days, a buzzing vibe, a desire to connect with others more. More socializing and celebrating, connecting with the expansiveness of life herself. Spend plenty of time consciously enjoying the precious moments of life.

Monthly, this may be when the moon is full.

Personally, and for many women, my cycle can change depending on where I am in the world, and what I have been experiencing in my healing journey. It can be helpful to become aware of your cycle, your rhythm and your season, to help you become more in tune with your mood, desires, emotions, motivation (or lack of!), remember every-body is different!

PURPOSE PROMPTS

Track your monthly cycle

Each day, for at least one month (aim for three months or more to get an accurate gauge), track your mood, your energy, and your emotions, reactions, and desires to "do" versus to "be." Begin to notice where in your body's monthly cycle you are. If you have a monthly period, "day one" of your month begins on the first day of your bleed. If you do not have a period, begin to observe your monthly cycle using the moon, starting at the new moon (although it works if you start at the full moon, too). Sometimes, just having the awareness of your monthly cycle, how you respond to the world on any given day, and where you are in your cycle, can be enough to reclaim power over your energy and emotions.

I used to feel super emotional about two or three times a month, and my emotions would trip me up. I would wake up agitated with no real reason as well and become angry much more easily. When I began tracking my cycle, I could see exactly where in the month this was, and that in itself began to shift it. It now happens once every few months, and I have the wisdom and intelligence around it to not behave in a way I might regret later, instead processing any stored emotions wanting to be expressed with a good cry and without projecting it onto my husband.

Start tracking today, and then on your "day one," begin to observe exactly whereabouts in your monthly rhythm things happen for you.

Observe your yearly rhythm

Just like your monthly rhythm, you'll also have a yearly rhythm. We are cyclical beings, and the range of our emotions may differ, but they are still all present. You may notice in winter that you tend to feel a bit lower than in summer. If you live in a climate that doesn't have physical seasons as such, you'll still likely have a yearly rhythm. I've had clients who are from the northern hemisphere but living in the southern hemisphere and vice-versa, and they notice their yearly rhythm matches the seasons of their birth-hemisphere. You may like to physically track each month by taking note or writing a summary of what you have experienced in energy and emotions. Or it may be very apparent to you without even needing to do this.

Understanding your natural rhythms and cycles can become a superpower when it comes to healing, self-discovery, and setting yourself up for greater success, happiness, and enjoyment of life. Do not underestimate the power of this.

Set up systems and/or support to help you honor your rhythms

This may be having conversations with your friends, family, or team, and getting them on board with any changes you will begin to implement in your household or business, especially in the "winter" phases of your cycle.

This may be asking for help or getting creative with a group of friends to become each other's support network.

Be creative. Ask yourself what would make your life a lot easier and begin to create solutions from there.

See what you can achieve by listening, feeling, BEING.

Life flows when you do.

Trust your own rhythm and cycles and experiences above what others experience or what you may read here. This is simply a guide, and you tapping into your own rhythm is much more powerful.

STUDENT OF LIFE

I live a slow-paced life.

This is how I achieve more.

I don't do busy.
I don't force.
Or hustle.

My life is full.

Lots of the time, it's filled with space.

I spend lots of time within.

I constantly expand and stretch my comfort zone.

I give a lot.

And I honor my energy and commitment to my path.

I admit my mistakes and change entire belief systems if they no longer serve me, opting to see life in new ways, from new perspectives.

I learn.

I do not avoid my pain. I face it. I sit with it. I process it. I purge it. I expand with it.

I look my shadows in the eye, even when my whole body wants to run, or I find myself trying to distract myself.

I'm a student of life.

Others ask me to teach them my ways.

But my secret is that I simply help you unlock your own.

To say goodbye to the old ways that don't work.

The societal constructs of busy-ness, hustle, and force.

To align with your highest experience and mission in this thing called life.

Abundance, bliss, and positive impact are the by-product.

LIVING FROM THE HEART

"Even after all this time, the sun never says to the earth 'you owe me.' Look what happens with a love like that, it lights the whole sky."

- Hafiz.

I commit to expanding my heart and truly living with love.

Without this, nothing else matters.

When I was at a business retreat in Canada, we had to do an exercise where half the group was blindfolded, and the other half of us—without blindfolds—had to walk into the room where our peers were standing, blind to what was happening, and give one person the biggest hug of our lives.

The song "All of Me" by John Legend was playing loudly as I walked over to my new friend to give her the biggest hug I could. I heard her emotion; she had no idea who was hugging her. In that moment, so innocently intimate, vulnerable, and close to this woman who was so openly expressing the deep emotion of receiving, I realized I was so far in my own head. Disconnected from my own emotions, disconnected from my heart. It was like I was trying to THINK my way into the frequency of love.

I realized in that moment, I'd been hiding under a mask of "heart" that was largely ruled by my mind—in fear of giving too much, being too much, or being inappropriate or hurt in my receiving. I thought I already gave so much, but I realized from this moment, I was giving from my head more than my heart... thinking my way through acts of love.

True giving is so profound and deep and really is an all-encompassing energy that infinitely flows and renews.

I felt shame at how much I thought I'd been giving, but in reality, I'd been so closed in my heart. I held such a fear of being hurt, uncomfortable, pained, rejected, told off... things I was still carrying from past wounds, so I had emotionally and unconsciously chosen to close my heart as it was easier that way.

Still blindfolded and embracing each other, intuitively, she felt my closed heart. She held me tighter. Hugged me deeper.

"It's safe," I heard.

I opened my heart and let the tears fall down my cheeks.

"It's safe."

I no longer need to keep my heart closed. I no longer need to fear the hurt from the past. I no longer have a need for the walls. I no longer have a need for amour. I no longer need to walk on eggshells in my own being.

"It's safe."

Right afterwards, I shared my experience with the whole group. I expressed my shame, my awareness of how I had been afraid of truly giving to my loved ones, afraid to tell them how much I truly loved them, cared for them, and appreciated them. In those moments, everything changed.

I realized that I can love so much more.

I am ready to open my heart and truly receive while simultaneously giving.

Truly receive.
Truly give.

The two-way tap of utmost importance to truly live from our hearts.
Giving and receiving.
Self-love is equally as important as loving others.
Receiving love is equally as important as giving love.
Vulnerability takes a whole new meaning.
What would happen if our whole world learned how to live from our hearts? I no longer need to wear the armor of masks. I allow myself to be seen fully and wholly. I am the light of the Universe. I carry the flame of eternal love. I allow it to show, to shine.

I release the belief that I'm too much. It is my truth that the expression of my full self is beautiful.
I am loved, and it is safe to be me.

I am safe to be me.
I am safe to be me.
I am safe to be me.

THE MOST IMPORTANT WORD IN YOUR HEALING JOURNEY

"Thanks, but no thanks. Not this time. Not for me. So kind of you to ask, but unfortunately not. Wish I could, but I won't. Not vibing with it. Doesn't align. Nope. Hmmmmm, nooooo. Nup. Na. No. No. No. No."

-The most important word in your healing journey
and a few ways to say it

I literally had to practice saying "No."

When I was changing my life, I remember driving to a party in my early days of sobriety practicing saying "No" out loud. I had to learn how to feel it in my body. I can distinctly remember feeling what it felt like in my solar plexus, when I tapped into this power that I had just discovered.

It was like a new weapon I unleashed. Had I really gone this long letting myself be taken advantage of, controlled, manipulated, used, abused, and just nodded, and allowed it?

Fuck. Yes. I had.

Wow. I never truly learned how to activate my sacred no-muscle.

Realizing it was a trauma response to simply agree and be submissive to life, I had a shit ton of healing and self-loving to do. Such a simple word. So many different outcomes it could have resulted in. Yet here I was, after a lifetime of yes's—even in times, I really meant no—left to deal with the consequences, reclaiming my position as captain of my body, leader of my life, director of my decisions, and learning how to make peace with the past.

When choosing a life of your highest path, strengthening your no-muscle isn't a luxury, it's a necessity. For me, it started with learning how to say no to booze and drugs, even when people were doing lines and offering them to me. It then mapped over to my mission and business, when friends thought I was just "home all the time" and couldn't understand why I wouldn't hang out with them on their days off. I had to be strong in my no to stay focused on my mission.

I didn't always get it right (still don't), and would still find myself making hefty investments, saying yes to collaborations or partnerships that weren't fully aligned, and in situations where I left thinking WTF, all because of my desire to appease others in those moments, afraid of standing my ground and outweighing my desire to honor my own "No".

It is in those moments we give away our power. And energetically imbalanced, the Universe will always bring us lessons to bring us back into balance. Sometimes it's a gentle nudge, other times, it's a full-blown breakdown, and other times still, it's an entire life transformation and ego shedding like never before. Either way, we have got to come back into balance and harmony with ourselves at some point. And learning how to honor your no, is a massive part of it.

It might look like:
No, I don't wanna go to that party.
OR: No I don't wanna sleep with that man / woman.
OR: This job isn't right for me. The pay is GREAT, but something just feels off.
OR: This relationship is comfortable, but I'm sure I deserve to be treated better.

It can be subtle, or full blown. It's up to us to get really good at listening, connecting, and trusting, without it needing to make sense right away, if at all.

The idea that we have to be superwoman or a "yes man" is an outdated fashion of which we're still experiencing the dregs. To reclaim full sovereignty of our lives and bodies, and unhook from collective control, manipulation, and fear systems, we must learn to say "no" far more frequently than we're used to doing.

It is so easy for us to want to help others, to validate them, to be a source for their happiness. Either consciously or not. When we do this, we enable another being to seek outside themselves for their own power, their own happiness and healing.

How often do you spend time with someone, and they say, "I feel so good being around you!"

Yet, you're left feeling drained, and they can't wait to see you again to get their next dose of happiness.

I used to see this all the time in relationships. And I enjoyed being needed. I enjoyed being a source of people's happiness. The only thing I didn't realize then was that I wasn't actually helping them realize they have their own source of happiness within. I was enabling behavior that disconnected them from their own power, and simultaneously, giving away my own. When we rely on another or external things for our own validation, we're preventing ourselves from owning our true power and connecting with the parts of us within who are already whole.

As we step into new levels of sovereignty and self-responsibility, we know that when we validate our own needs, we don't have that neediness to be seen and heard by others. We see ourselves; we love ourselves; we give ourselves what we need.

We're tapping into releasing co-dependency and coming back to inter-dependency here, which is a whole subject in itself. When we are whole and full, we have an energy of inter-dependency and don't "need" to be validated by others. We self-validate and know our worth, regardless of whether someone compliments us or criticizes us.

As one of my teachers shared with me, "When we say 'no' to someone else, we say 'yes' to ourselves."

If you know you're here on a mission to create a better earth and a better humanity, learning to say no is going to be one of the best gifts you can give yourself as you create a new way of being for the world, starting first with your own life.

If you're saying "yes" when you really mean "no" to the requests of others, what are you missing out on in embodying your own highest potential?

YOUR "NO" IS SACRED

Saying yes because I didn't want to upset someone, or I didn't want to make them feel rejected, has put me in some ridiculously compromising situations, including being in relationships with men when I actually didn't want to, letting strangers stay with my husband and me on vacation because they didn't have anywhere to stay, giving away client sessions for free after giving too much, and people expecting more of me, having people join my travels when I wanted to be solo, investing thousands of dollars into personal development just because I didn't want to upset the person if I said "No..."

All these situations left me feeling depleted, used, frustrated ,and annoyed—at first, at the person "taking advantage of me" (as I used to put it), and later on, when taking full responsibility for myself and my actions, towards myself.

I had been living under this spell that we need to do as others ask, or else, be told off. My inner child still very much running the show.

While it's great to understand where our wounds, which prevent us from living in full alignment, have come from, it's more important to change the behaviors. To change behaviors, we must also unhook from the unresolved emotions or change the mindset that is keeping us looped in old patterns.

If we have awareness of something, and don't change it, heal it, or shift it, we're willingly choosing to oblige our old patterns. When we oblige our old patterns, nothing changes.

We don't change, and we don't make the impact in the world that we came here to make.

For me, not saying no enough, or perhaps saying yes too quickly and then either going back on my word, or reluctantly following through because I don't want to go back on my word, is something I still work on.

Our souls know if something is in alignment for us or not.

It's not our job to decide if something is a "yes" or a "no," if it's in alignment for us or not. Our souls tell us through our bodies and the way we feel. It's up to us to listen and follow through with that guidance.

We're human. We're going to make mistakes. Sometimes, we make the same mistakes in different ways as we delve deeper into the truth of all that we are.

When we remember that "yes" and "no" are equally weighted—yes isn't good and no isn't bad, or vice versa—we allow ourselves to approach life with deeper empowerment, groundedness, and strength.

Learning our yes's and no's is a fundamental element of truly breaking rules and living the life you were born to live.

PURPOSE PROMPTS

What things are you currently doing, or have done in the past, that have gone against your inner-no?

_____

_____

_____

_____

Why do you feel you said yes, or nothing at all, instead of no?

_____

_____

_____

_____

If you had said no, or were to say no in the future, what may happen?

_____

_____

_____

_____

Remember, you are not responsible for how people react when you set your boundaries or honor your "No." You ARE responsible for your happiness, your energy, your time, and what you give energy and focus to. Next time something arises that you feel your inner no speaking to you, what will you do?

_____

_____

_____

_____

Why is this important to you?

_____

_____

_____

What will happen if you do not honor your no?

_____

_____

_____

_____

YOU'RE NOT A DOORMAT

It's great to love everyone. It really is. I love every human who walks this planet.

However, for most of my life, this was a detriment. It meant that I let myself be taken advantage of, maintained hazy boundaries, and kept people in my life who weren't healthy to have around.

You can be spiritual and assertive.

We are human. We have ego and we have boundaries.

I let boys cheat on me and forgave them, thinking I was being loving by giving them another chance.

I let friends bully me and forgave them, thinking I was being loving by giving them unlimited chances.

I let acquaintances gossip behind my back, forgave them, and naively kept spending time with them.

This goes beyond loving every human and now becomes a matter of self-respect.

I used to think I was loving and trusting and just seeing the best in everyone.

Forgetting what self-love meant in the process.

Setting strong boundaries isn't unloving.

It's a sign of self-respect and self-love.

It also gives others an opportunity to reflect on their behavior and change.

If it weren't for people and boyfriends setting strong boundaries or releasing me from their life, I wouldn't have had the opportunity to see the implications of my actions on others and would have kept repeating the same patterns.

I always do a "self-reflection" when I'm feeling hurt, upset, heartbroken, or in times of conflict.

It's not from a place of blame, but I ask myself questions like, "How did I contribute to this? What can I take responsibility for here? What can I change? How would I show up differently if I'm in the same situation again?"

Just as you don't want to only point fingers and blame someone else, you also want to make sure you don't take responsibility for everything when that's not the case. The pendulum can swing too far that way, too, and I used to also find myself taking full responsibility for disagreements, arguments, and conflict just to make the other person feel better.

If you make a mistake, own it.

Apologize, and make new choices next time.

If you ever feel like something is missing from life, or that you always look to things outside yourself hoping "the next thing" holds the secret answer to what you've been looking for all along, odds are, it won't. Perhaps, like I did, you look to alcohol, drugs, men (or women), clothes, another five pounds to lose, the next job, next vacation, next project, new pet, or a new home, believing it's going to give you the happiness you crave.

Then, remember... all your answers are within you.

Each experience, each situation you find yourself in, is an opportunity to grow, to get to learn who you are, to know yourself more. When you look at life as such, you'll begin to find the keys of inner freedom, peace, and happiness. You'll see your own courage and strength, the resilience you embody.

And ultimately, you'll feel your own love. You'll experience true happiness from within.

Just as emotions hold the key to deeper layers of ourselves, boundaries are also essential for us to discover more of ourselves, to heal what's ours and understand ourselves on a deeper level.

If we try to "love" everyone when it means disrespecting ourselves, we shut off a part our truth. When we shut off our truth, we shut off our capacity to truly flourish in the unique divinity that we all are.

You can still be spiritual and assertive.

You can still love and forgive people and no longer have a relationship with them.

You can still be the strongest person you know and feel every emotion that comes into your body.

You have so much love in your heart.

You love the world and its inhabitants so much. Let that be your permission to know you're a good person. Let that be your permission to know you are such a loving soul.

Let that be your permission to operate from a place of love, in particular, self-love.

You're not a doormat. You don't have to tolerate people treating you like one.

PURPOSE PROMPTS

If you're operating from a place of fear (fear of not being liked, fear of hurting someone, even if they are hurting you, fear of letting go, fear of conflict, etc.) ask yourself:

If I were not afraid in this situation, what would I do?

_____

_____

_____

_____

If I were to truly love and respect myself, how would I respond differently?

_____

_____

_____

_____

If you notice you have a fear of not being liked, or of conflict, ask yourself where this came from? How old were you when this started? What happened in your life that impacted this? If you were to meet that younger version of you again right now, what would you say to them?

_____

_____

_____

_____

YOUNGER-SELF HEALING EXERCISE

- Close your eyes and visualize the younger version of yourself in the situation you are ready to let go of. You may also like to find a photograph of yourself around a similar age of the situation you are healing from.

- Let this version of you know you're here for them, that you love them, and that you know exactly what they're going through because you are them.

- Ask what she or he needs from you now.

- Listen as you intuitively hear, sense, or just know what they will share with you. Perhaps they are wanting to be acknowledged in what they are feeling. Perhaps they want to "say" something they've never said to anyone before. Perhaps they just want to be loved and accepted exactly as they are.

- Give him or her a hug, thank them for their strength, put your arm around them, and be the person they needed. Tell them you love them, you are here with them, they are loveable, worthy, and enough, and that you are so proud of them.

- Continue with this until it feels complete. Some situations may require more time and attempts to fully let go. There's no right or wrong. You can't rush your healing.

- Invite that version of you back into your heart. Let them know it is safe now, and that you are looking after them, giving them what they need. They are worthy and loved and more than enough, exactly as they are.

- Next time you look in a mirror, see beyond your current physical appearance. See the younger version of you. Look into their eyes and say, "I see you, I honor you, I love you".

AND SO SHE ROCKED THE WORLD WITH HER CONFIDENCE

And so she rocked the world with her confidence.

She took herself by storm.

She soared beyond her wildest dreams, and her new life was born.

She challenged the status quo.

She strummed to the tune of her intuition.

She knew there was more to life and more that she could grow.

She won't back down, she won't take no for an answer.

She answers to no one but the divine, and that my love, is perfectly quite fine.

She's wild, she's brave, she's a rebel with a cause.

She chooses love over fear, heart over ego.

She smiles freely, especially when she honors her boundaries.

Love is her destiny. Her birthright. Her truth.

She sees the light in the dark, the compassion in the pain.

She knows that no two individuals are the same.

Yet she preaches we are one.

For we are one.

But we are not the same.

That is our beauty, our strength, yet also our pain.

Let our differences be our pride, not our shame.

Shine, my love.

Rise above.

Let your truth be heard, first and foremost by your heart.

We are one.

I want you to be you and me to be me.

When we agree on that, then we'll be free.

There's so much love in my heart, I wish you could see.

For it is not "You and I," it is "We."

Sister, brother, it's our time.

Rise, we are needed.

Our light, our love. We have a mission.

I can't wait for the day we unite, and we all say,

"mission accomplished".

I'll see you there.

But until then, come back to

Your truth.

My truth. Our truth.

YOU DON'T HAVE TO EXPLAIN YOURSELF

You don't have to explain yourself.

To anyone.

Especially regarding your success, abundance, blessings, and good fortune.

We seem to live in this world of having to justify or seek approval that our heart's desires, visions, dreams, and blessings are okay to have—like we're waiting for someone to give us permission to live our most magnificent life.

That we are worthy of our success.

Here's the deal. Success, abundance, love, joy, peace, freedom, and total liberation are your birthright as a human being, born into this human life. The very fact you are here is the only permission you need, the only explanation required when pondering whether you can truly live your dreams.

You are a divine, sovereign being. All your happenings in life are between you and the Universe.

There's no need to explain or justify your happy relationship, your thriving business, your lifestyle.

Regardless of whether it has come easily for you, or you've worked your ass off to achieve it.

The need for justification, clarification, explanation, or validation comes from many places, both societal and individual, and is often subtly, or not so subtly imposed by external factors throughout your life.

You might notice an unconscious self-sabotage playing out in your life, disguised as an underlying feeling of unworthiness, lack of self-belief, or not wanting to "outshine" others. Ever been cut down by your peers when celebrating your achievements? Consider this might be subconsciously playing out when you're setting out to achieve success and rather than being "cut down" again, it's "easier" not to shine too brightly, not achieve too much, not dream too big, and not go after your dreams, in case others get upset by it. You can't control others' beliefs and opinions, but they are not any reason to keep yourself small, and they are certainly not a reason to need to explain or justify your dreams.

Whatever you have experienced in the past, you are able to rewire your core beliefs so that you are literally wired for abundance, success, and a magnificent life.

And for now, please know that you deserve all the happiness in the world.

You deserve the loving relationship, the successful business or career, the dream lifestyle, the ultimate happiness. You deserve it all.

All of your unique talents, gifts, intellect, wisdom, growth, and development are aspects of your journey that make you uniquely you, and no one can take that away from you. You don't have to explain yourself to anyone. You deserve it all.

There's no need to fear being greedy. If you understand the difference between entitlement and deserving and worthy, you'll know how to stay humble, grateful, and respectful, and honor all you have with a sense of compassion, kindness, grace, and responsibility.

If you worked hard to get to where you are today, have gratitude for all things that have helped you get to where you are.

Without explanation.

If you've been born into "success," have gratitude for this. Have humility in this and have grace in this.

Without explanation.

You know that you'll do your part of service for the highest good of the planet with all your fortune and love. You don't need to justify all that you have to anyone else.

Your relationship with life is between you and the Universe. No one else. Not another human being.

Yes, absolutely, give whatever you desire from a place of love and a full cup. But give nothing from a place of obligation or manipulated energy.

I remember when I started seeing "success" (whatever this truly means?!). People would say, "Oh you're so lucky, getting to travel and being able to work whenever you want, from anywhere you want, and for your amazing marriage...." and I would come back with, "Yes, but it's been so hard to get here. I chose this life, but it's taken the darkness of my shadows to make this happen. It's been very challenging."

Somehow, I was hoping that if they could see something negative in my "success," they would leave me alone, or perhaps approve of me and my lifestyle.

I would dim my light, sometimes switching it right off, hoping this would help explain myself.

NO MORE.

I know how hard I've worked to get to where I am. I know what it's truly taken. But that's between me and the Universe.

I now share with people when they ask with a genuine desire to learn, with my clients, or close friends. But no longer do I feel the need to justify, validate, or give anything away just for the sake of feeling I have to explain myself to those who "don't get it."

You might have experienced this, too.

I'm pretty sure you have. Most people I work with have fallen into this trap as they start to rise. We're pretty good as humans at accidentally placing our own expectations of how life should be onto others.

It's called projection. We project our beliefs onto others and place our own expectations, judgments, opinions, and desires onto them. We might even project our jealousy or resentment, anger or feelings of not being enough ourselves, onto the lives of others.

This is not okay. This is low-vibrational, and the opposite of what it is to be liberated.

Break the rules of current human society by letting people be free.

Don't cast your own judgments onto others. Let others decide how they want to live. Let others decide what's right for them or not.

Free others and free yourself.

Don't expect others to explain themselves, and please know that you never have to explain yourself, to anyone, other than the creator.

This is your life, your soul path, your spiritual journey, your growth, your experience, your divinity. The time has come to feel full, whole, complete, and loved in the knowledge that your life is between you, your soul, and your own spiritual guidance.

You are free.

Be free.

Be freed.

BREAK THE RULES

To create a life you're madly in love with, it's going to require you to shatter some of the boxes and rules you've unconsciously been living by.

Fuck the rules.

You weren't born to dress to the fashions of society.

You were born to create a new way, design a new movement.

You're here to bring color to the drab grey that dresses the masses.

Inject music into the silent groans of mediocrity.

You're here to rip off the patches hiding the holes and confront the flaws holding on by a thread.

Fuck the rules.

You're the designer of your movement.

Clothed in your own fashion.

Lead the way as you strut by example down the runway of your life.

Bold changes in fashion start with a bold designer.

LIVING YOUR SOUL'S MISSION

When you look at your whole life up until this moment, and look at all the lessons, experiences, interactions, breakdowns, breakthroughs, education, qualifications, healings, heartaches, strength-provoking moments... they begin to add up pretty quickly!

You realize you're "more qualified" than you think (or than society might lead you to think!) to be doing what you were put on this planet to do.

Right now, many leaders are creating things that haven't actually been done before, meaning that there is no qualification to complete... your life experience IS the qualification.

Giving yourself permission to break the rules, and knowing you are here to make a difference, is the first step.

I always say to my clients, "Courage comes before confidence!"

Of course, it's easy to say "Yes, I'm here to make a big difference in the world," and another thing to embody this.

Often, the embodiment process is one of letting go of all limitations picked up through life—ancestrally, socially, and collectively, and even from past lives.

The more you can FEEL the magnificence and magnitude of your soul mission on a cellular level, the easier it is to magnetize the right people, opportunities, and resources for you to make the impact you are here to make.

It's a funny weight to bear, knowing that you're here to do something. And like trying to scratch an invisible itch, you don't stop until you know what that "something" is.

Like you, I've always felt like there's something more I have gotta be doing in life.

Always jumping from one thing to the next—relationships, jobs, houses, travel, holiday, outfits, courses—always learning, moving, and seeking.

Only a few years into my healing journey, I was having a conversation with some girlfriends who I had known since high school. I was sharing how one day, "When I'm running my own company, these are the rules I'm going to impose (or rather, remove) for how I want my team to show up, to remove anything that restricts their sense of freedom or obligation and help them tap into THEIR best way of living."

What's funny about that is that I was still working in corporate and had no idea what SORT of company I'd be running, and even more, that I'd be running my own company less than a year later from that moment.

When it comes to BREAKING rules, I believe the most important RULE to remember is that there ARE no rules to begin with.

It's about breaking all societal beliefs, cultural expectations, and familial traditions when they're not serving us, or helping us expand, evolve, and create a better world.

Breaking rules is about REMEMBERING how to dream again.

To speak into existence your soul's very desires.

To share from your heart, despite the risk of being ridiculed.

It's about remembering your ever-expanding nature and removing all boxes that you've found yourself accidentally placed in, whether they were self-imposed or not.

Boxes and conformity are not our natural state.

Conformity in society is like going to a restaurant, seeing lots of wonderful dishes on the menu, yet when your order arrives, while aesthetically pleasing, it lacks substance, flavor, and that kind of more-ish feeling you hope to have in your meal when dining out.

It's like, when you look at society on the surface, everything's fine. But then you wonder why it's so hard to find deep connections with other human beings. Why conversations feel flat and dull, and why, while you crave hearing the dreams, desires, and deepest experiences of your fellow-human beings, you're met with hearing all about the local weather and current council issues.

Being a rule breaker means challenging conformity. Going deep. Speaking about love, kindness, and compassion, intertwined with your theories on the very existence of humanity and the universe, instead of putting up with gossip, judgment, and what next summer's fashion statement will be.

This is where connection is.

This is where we find our purpose.

This is where we begin to create a world of love, peace, freedom, and abundance.

When we meet each day, showing up as the fullest expression of ourselves.

But it's up to you, to us, the ones who think like this, who see the world differently than our peers, governments, and societies.

It's up to us to wake up, rise and shine, and remind others how to do the same.

To remove the fear of being human.

To remove the fear of expressing emotion, talking about what we actually care about.

To give this life our all, our everything, all of us.

Most people don't even know that there's more to life and themselves than they experience on a daily basis. They've forgotten how to remember the true magnificence and unlimited, abundant, and infinite being that they are.

Humanity, on the large part, has forgotten how to think for itself.

We're glued to our screens, the news, and whatever medium we can get our hands on to look for the answers all of us are silently craving—the answers our conscious minds don't even know we're asking questions about.

We're so filled with the idea that our existence is in our jobs, money, house, societal status, the amount of tequila we drank on the weekend, the guys or girls we've shagged, the size of our wardrobes, and how many pairs of shoes we own.

We're so caught up in enlarging our boobs and lips and butts that we've forgotten to enlarge the things that truly matter...

Our hearts, our souls, our brilliance.

I WISH YOU KNEW HOW STRONG YOU TRULY ARE

I wish you knew how strong you truly are.

I wish you weren't afraid of the unknown but rather, trusted your deep knowing.

The deep knowing inside yourself that knows you're cut out for so much more.

That your greatest potential is lying dormant inside you.

Like a lion that's been tamed for the zoo. Those lions kind of act like lions, but they lack the fierce wildness that makes them so special, yet still lays deep within. The lion within you is ready to be unleashed.

Take a leap of faith. Go after what you truly desire. Your deepest desires are a leap away. You don't know how to get there. And that's okay. The first leap will lead to the second and so on.

Your life matters. Your life is designed to be large. Stop playing small to fit in a box. The world needs your strength. The strength to be yourself in a society that squishes us so strongly into little, teeny boxes. Those teeny boxes keep us from doing anything too outrageous: like being our authentic selves.

Because imagine the world if we were all strong enough to be our authentic selves. Working for causes that truly matter.

The causes that truly matter to you. Is it climate change? Animal warfare? LGBTQ+ rights? Spiritual alignment? Health? Wellness? Paper plane enthusiast movement?

Imagine how incredible the world would truly be if we spent our energy on becoming our most authentic selves and living our best lives, filled with our biggest passions, living for every single moment and none of this "OMG can't wait till the weekend" business EVER again.

Discover and unleash your most authentic self. I dare you.

PURPOSE PROMPTS

What are all the things that make you brilliant? If you find this challenging to answer, begin by reflecting on things people have thanked you for, or what a loved one or a stranger might have lovingly said to you, perhaps about the way you treated another person, or something you'd said or done that positively impacted someone.

_____

_____

_____

_____

_____

_____

_____

_____

_____

_____

_____

_____

_____

Now, what are five life events you've experienced that have contributed to shaping who you are today?

_____

_____

_____

_____

_____

What are the main lessons you learned through each experience? How have they helped you become who you are today? Do these lessons feel empowering? If not, how can you see them in a new light and find gifts of strength, connection, boundaries, confidence, courage, love.....?

_____

_____

_____

_____

_____

_____

_____

_____

How would you like to use these experiences, gifts, or lessons to help others?

_____

_____

_____

_____

If you could impact the planet or humanity in one way, what would that be?

_____

_____

_____

_____

_____

I BELIEVE IN MIRACLES

"You'll see it when you believe it"
--- on the wall of a cafe in Canggu, Bali

I remember the exact moment I first started TRULY believing in miracles.

I was 11 years old.

It was summertime, and we'd just come back from a three-week family vacation in Mahia—a little beach town in the Hawke's Bay, New Zealand, where we went camping every year.

I was due to start my form two year in a few weeks, at the same school I'd been at the year prior, and the year after I'd be heading off to high school for form three.

My parents had tried to enrol me into private schools since the age of 4, but I'd never got into any of them, meanwhile some of my friends went off to private school after primary school and I joined another group in public school.

My parents were devastated when they found out I hadn't gotten into private school. They never said anything, but I could feel it.

Because of where we lived, it also meant the only high school I was able to go to was the lowest decile public school in our area.

Teen pregnancy, drugs, and truancy were the norm there.

I'd been to visit the school once when I was playing flute in my school orchestra. I distinctly remember looking forward to getting out of there as soon as our band had finished playing.

So here I was, arriving back home in summer ready and excited for the new year ahead, my last year at the public school before going off to high school and becoming a teenager.

One of the first things my Mom did was check the voice messages on the landline to see who called while we'd been away.

LIBBY!

I heard her calling out to me.

Libby! You've got an interview at Saints College!

Saints was the semi-private school I hadn't gotten into the year before. One of my best friends from primary school had gotten in, and I'd already met some of her friends who went there.

Immediately, I felt the excitement.

The private school had called and left a message inviting me to an interview only days away from the time we got home and checked the message.

An interview! For private school!

But.... there was a catch. Two other girls were being interviewed, and there was only one spot.

My Mom told me not to get my hopes up, but I couldn't help myself.

PRIVATE SCHOOL!

I got everything ready. I remember creating a portfolio of "me"— my first "CV." It included some of my school work, a letter from our church, and a letter from me that I had written to the principal as to why I'd be the best candidate for that one spot.

On the day of the interview with the principal, I put on my Sunday Best...
That spot was mine! It had to be!

I didn't want to go to the other high school! Mainly because I could see how upset it was making my parents.

In the days leading up to the interview, I could feel my Mom's excitement. I heard her telling some friends "I can't believe it... if we'd come home ANY later from vacation we would have missed out!"

Not only that, but we moved that year and the phone number the school had on file from when I didn't get in was registered to our old address.

Rather than doing the usual change of phone number when you moved, my parents went through the process of keeping the same number.

If they had changed phone numbers like most people did when moving house those days, the phone book wouldn't have been updated to reflect our change in address or change in phone number, meaning the school wouldn't have been able to get in touch and leave a voice message as they did.

The little details that lined up to getting that interview were ALL miracles in themselves!

I KNEW with every part of me that I was going to get that spot at that school.

I imagined myself putting on the uniform. I imagined myself going there each day. I imagined my new group of friends.

The interview went well, or so I thought.

I found out afterwards that one of the other girls who received an interview couldn't make the interview, and the other one decided to stay at the school she was already in.

I BECAME THE ONLY CANDIDATE! THE SPOT WAS MINE!

The energy and excitement I felt coming from my parents celebrating me getting into this school... it also meant my two younger sisters were also able to be easily granted a place, too, my middle sister started three years later, and my youngest sister started six years later.

It also meant my parents had to work harder and longer hours than ever to earn more money to be able to send me here. The gratitude I have for them when they had three daughters all at that school paying all three tuitions is immense. What they sacrificed to make that possible is enormous and something I hold an incredible amount of gratitude for.

All of the mini miracles that happened to allow the miracle of me going to a good school changed the trajectory of my life *forever*.

From that moment onward, I not only BELIEVED in miracles, but through first-hand experience, I KNEW, with every single part of my being, that the Universe, God, Source, Creator was 100% looking out for me, and that I was ALWAYS taken care of.

That is still the same level of faith I live with each and every day and is the foundation for how I created my dream life and business. It's why I know the same is possible for you, too.

You don't need to experience anything as dramatic as that to have faith and belief in miracles.

Look at how you're even still alive today.

Look at how you have eyes to read this.

How you have a heart that beats just for you, and cells all working with one goal in mind: KEEPING YOU ALIVE.

Our very EXISTENCE as human beings is the real reason I believe in miracles, and from this moment forward, I encourage you to look for miracles every single day. When you open your eyes, and your heart, you'll see the mini miracles continuously unfolding before your eyes.

PURPOSE PROMPTS

Write out all the times you remember experiencing a miracle, no matter how big or small.

_____

_____

_____

_____

_____

_____

_____

_____

For the next week (or month if you're serious about creating miracles), open a new "note" in your phone, or keep a journal with you, and each time a mini miracle happens, take note of it. At the end of each day, look at all the miracles that have happened. Do this each week, and each month, and you'll literally SEE the magic always happening around you, and begin becoming a magnet for even more.

PART FOUR: SHINING LIGHT ON YOUR SHADOWS

YOU CANNOT HAVE LIGHT WITHOUT DARK

To begin living your life's purpose and to live a life of organic happiness, it is important to know and love our authentic, truest, whole selves. Not just the desirable parts of us we try to show more of to the world, but all of us. Even the less desirable facets of our consciousness. The more love we embody, the more love ripples through the web of life, through humanity. If you want to embody more love, more light, you must look at the places in your consciousness that are NOT of love or light, things hidden, or suppressed away in the shadows, to release them.

As you'll remember from the depths of your soul:
Healing and happiness is not the absence of darkness, but rather an observation and understanding of the darkness, of your own shadows, without attachment to them, or judgment of them.
When you commit to living your life's purpose and soul mission, and you go all in, the universe brings everything you need to hold a stronger container for everything you're calling in.

Sometimes this process isn't exactly fun, but there's no suffering in this shadow because "It is," not "I am."

You can experience depth of emotion without adopting the emotion as "Me."

And you can experience the emotion without projecting it onto others; simply letting it be an experience of the human.

Your business, your money, your relationships—it's all related to your inner beliefs that you've adopted about the world, in this lifetime and others, as well as ancestral beliefs, combined with a deeper soul knowing.

All of these beliefs hold frequencies and codings in your human template, in a beautifully holistic way.

Want to make more money? Go within.
Want to expand your business? Go within.
Want to connect to the Source more? Go within.
Want nourishing relationships? Go within.
Want more freedom and happiness? Go within.

Your answers are inside, and you are here creating the new earth through all the actions you take and new levels of self you embody.

Right now, light is being shed on all misalignments. Listen and observe and commit to rising.

You are loved, you are guided, you are supported.

THE ROLE OF HEALERS

Healers—or lightworkers—have come to the planet to bring more light.

We're often born into families, environments, and locations that hold much pain, trauma, and darkness.

Addictions, abuse, and mental health issues often plague our family lines.

Healers can often feel like the black sheep, and can head down a dark path themselves, becoming entangled in these patterns.

Most often, they'll come to a crossroads and realize the dark path is not what they're here on the planet to do.

(I always knew partying, drugging, and addiction wasn't the right path... I just didn't know another one. It became my identity, and was the only way I knew how to have fun... losing my mind).

Healer is a label placed on someone who has come to break ancestral patterns, be the change they desire to see in the planet, by going first and healing their own darkness.

Diving deep into the shadows of their unconscious.
Liberating themselves by dealing with their own demons.
Untangling themselves from collective patterns.
Going deep into ancestral lines and energy stored in the planet and the collective, to rise, and then to help others do the same.

Most healers I work with have encountered extreme traumas and darkness, and have developed deep resilience and use their darkness as strength to rise.

As human beings, removing any titles or labels, the deeper we dig, the more we can grow.

Through our growth, we create energetic roots in the earth, and from our hearts, flooded with the light straight from Source.

This light penetrates our entire energy system, and expands in the collective energy system, all the way into the Earth.

By looking at our darkness and shifting through it, processing it, being present with it, and through this, releasing it... we transmute what was dark, and through the process of experiencing it as it is, we're able to recalibrate each dark vibration to hold more light in our bodies.

The awareness of our darkness allows us to process it safely and not project it onto another human being.

Having awareness OF our darkness, our triggers, our inner demons, allows us to know ourselves more, and realize ALL our emotions and dark feelings are not that of another, but rather for us to experience, process, and eventually transmute into forgiveness, gratitude, compassion, and love.

There is no time limit on how long this takes.

Some wounds are bigger than others and take longer to process.

When we know we are not our darkness, but rather the awareness of our darkness, we remove the identity of the darkness and no longer see ourselves as dark.

If you can SEE and KNOW your darkness, well done.

You're holding more light than you give yourself credit for.

The darkness denies its darkness. Light shines awareness on the darkness and this is how we heal it.

If you're here, a rebel, black sheep, and rule breaker of your family... it's highly likely you see the world in a different way than those around you.

It's highly likely you have a gift of truth to bring forth.
Love is the only way to heal the dark.

Stay in your process.
Your work is honored.
Your ancestors thank you.
Future generations thank you.

Thank you for breaking cycles plaguing the planet with darkness.

Thank you for committing to holding more light.

Thank you for experiencing, with so much grace, the duality of the human experience, and letting it gift you so much strength.

SHINING LIGHT ON YOUR SHADOWS

"The shadow is a moral problem that challenges the whole ego-personality, for no one can become conscious of the shadow without considerable moral effort. To become conscious of it involves recognizing the dark aspects of the personality as present and real. This act is the essential condition for any kind of self-knowledge."

— *Carl Jung, Aion (1951)*

Do you have parts of you that you hope no one sees or no one discovers?

In the simplest of explanations and more often than not, that's your shadow.

We all have a shadow self, just not all of us are aware of it or conscious as to how we are blocking our best life because we've not yet met or accepted our shadows.

Have you ever been on the receiving end of someone yelling at you for apparently no reason? In the simplest of explanations and more often than not, that's their shadow.

Remember, we live in a world of duality.

Day / night.
Fear / love.
Happiness / sadness.
Rich / poor.
Healthy / ill.

Our shadows are our dark side.
Light / dark.

And whether we like it or not, we all have a shadow side.

The more aware we are of our shadows, the more we are able to love and transmute them, and ultimately, embody more love.
Many of us are actively trying to bring more love into the world and make the world a better place. To fully do this, it would be a huge mistake to only look at our love and light side. We disregard an entire aspect of ourselves and of humanity if we fail to look at our whole selves.

How do we get to know ourselves while trying to avoid whole aspects of ourselves?

When we understand the parts of us we try to hide, we know ourselves more fully. From here, we love ourselves more deeply. From here, through us embodying more self-love, we are no longer contributing to the very thing we were trying to heal in the first place, but rather through full acceptance and learning how to love the unlovable, we let go of the energetic weight many of us carry around every day and open up fully to the magic and miracles of life.

SHADOW ARCHETYPES

Here are some examples of how the shadow might be playing out in your life.

THE VILLAIN

Gaslighting. Projecting your own insecurities onto others.

When you're experiencing emotional outbursts frequently and you say to your partner, "Why are you so emotional all the time?"

Relationships often serve as mirrors of our own consciousness. When we're sitting in our Villain archetype, we like to deny this. The Villain doesn't want to be found out.

The antidote for the villain is looking at, and taking responsibility for, our part to play in a situation or relationship.

THE REBEL

Issues with authority.

Getting into an argument with the shop assistant, police officer, or someone of authority. If we're not aware of our Rebel Shadow Archetype, it can lead to arguments when someone of perceived authority gives us an instruction. I know this one well, and I often related to feeling like someone is trying to control me, coming from an unhealed part of me who had no control in unpleasant, often traumatic experiences.

The antidote to this is to heal and reclaim our power from situations where we had lack of control, especially around an authoritative figure in our lives.

THE PRINCESS

Being the victim.

Waiting to be saved. Waiting for someone else to come solve all of your problems. When we're in the Princess Shadow Archetype, we are never ever in the wrong. The Princess doesn't take responsibility for the situations they find themselves in and loves to blame others, the situation, anyone else involved: the cat, the weather. It's an "everyone else's fault but mine" kind of attitude.

The antidote for this is to take full responsibility for our lives and take charge of anything we are unhappy with.

THE IGNORANT ONE

Unconscious bias and prejudice.

The underlying attitudes and stereotypes that people unconsciously attribute to another person or group of people that affect how they engage with a person or group of people.

Racism, Sexism, Ageism, Classism, Homophobia, Nationalism, Religious prejudice are all examples of this shadow archetype.

The antidote for this is to educate ourselves, explore where we are holding judgements and stereotypes, and choose a more loving and inclusive perspective.

THE TYRANT

Your way or the highway, often at the expense of others.

Bullying others to feed a sense of self-importance. Being cruel, intentionally or unintentionally, to have control over people or a situation or environment. People may feel emotionally abused, or afraid to stand up for themselves around you.

The antidote for this is to listen to and understand those around you. To treat everyone with kindness and respect.

THE LOWER SELF

Sounds like your own inner dialogue but talks down to you.

The part of you that says things like "You can't do that," "Who do you think you are?" "You're not good enough," "You're not smart enough, good looking enough," "That's for others but not for you."

The antidote for this is to realize you don't have to believe your thoughts. When you hear your mind talking badly to you, find the strength in that moment to disagree with it, and choose a new, more helpful and loving thought that feels like you can believe it.

THE GRUDGE

Holding onto the past and being unwilling to forgive.

This could be towards yourself or another. Whenever we hold onto guilt, shame, resentment, anger, or wish ill will on another, it only causes more pain and suffering within us.

Forgiveness is the antidote to this.

THE BITCH

Tall poppy syndrome.

Jealous and cuts others down from their success, either in your own mind, or projected towards the person. It might sound like "Who does she think she is," "She's not even that special / talented / good," "I bet she's faking it."

The antidote to this is celebrating the success and happiness of others, it opens you up to more success and happiness yourself.

THE MANIPULATOR

Manipulative and controlling.

Do this or else X. Tries to control or manipulate others to get what they want, or take advantage of people or situations for personal gain.

The antidote to this, is to remember that everyone is a sovereign being and no one has control over another. Each human can make their own choices for themselves.

THE MESSIAH

Spiritual ego. Spiritual bypassing. Messiah Complex.

"I'm better than them because XYZ"...., pointing fingers, "They should do X" ...love and light over things and ignoring truth. When we are sitting in The Messiah Shadow Archetype, there can be an element or belief of "I am Holier Than Thou." It may look like gossiping or judging another. It may even look like ignoring a painful experience we've encountered and covering it up with "it's all good, it's forgiven," while unconsciously squishing the pain down and not actually dealing with it.

The antidote to this is to be real, true, and whole-heartedly honest with yourself about everything.

When we learn to love our darkness, we create a solid foundation within us.

To paraphrase the words of a healer I once worked with... "when we accept ourselves fully and love our shadows, it means if someone was to try to find things wrong with us, they will not succeed."

Not because you are perfect, but because you are aware of and understand your less "desirable" traits, you own your shadows. And you don't go around energetically vomiting on everyone because you are so self-aware and understand your responsibility of "holding" your light and your energy.

You're able to own your mistakes and be an energetically and emotionally responsible, mature human being.

You see, there's nothing wrong with you. Ever. Even the parts of you that you feel are wrong.

When you can learn to love all of you—the pieces of you that you wish you could hide forever—you own your mistakes and life is much easier. The first program I created in my business was called "Love Yourself Sober."

I discovered the only way I could heal my drinking problem was to find out why I had it in the first place. I spent several years discovering the root of the problem and learned to love those parts of me. I went deep into my traumas and experiences I had buried far below the surface of my memories. I learned to forgive myself. I learned to forgive my abusers. I learned how to make peace with the past, realizing I did the best I could with the information and knowledge I had. I realized I learned from my mistakes and would never make those same mistakes again. I began to love the versions of me who had done awful things, to myself and to others. I forgave those versions of me and thanked them for the lessons. I cut cords, I prayed, I journaled, I screamed, I got angry, I meditated, I danced, I exercised a lot to get all the stored emotional pain out of my body, I wrote letters and burned them, I cried...a lot. I felt a lot. I knew it would be easier to have a glass of wine to make it all go away, but I also knew that would be like putting a band-aid over a gaping wound. I had to let it all out. I knew this was the only way to heal.

I began to notice bouts of anxiety and depression becoming less and less frequent in my day-to-day life. I realized I no longer felt shame or guilt or remorse, or even regret for many of those experiences I was healing from. When I think back to some of the situations that brought up the deepest emotions of shame or remorse, I no longer have an emotional reaction, just love for those versions of me.

The only way to heal is to feel.
This is how I began to discover the secrets of Self Wealth.

THE TRUTH ABOUT SHADOW WORK

There's this perception that your shadow is bad, or evil.
Our shadows are simply the parts of our psyches that don't hold light,
and until we shine light on them, we aren't even aware of them.

The most important thing we can do as leaders of light on the planet
is to know ourselves as deeply and intimately as possible... ALL of us.
Even the parts we've tried to keep hidden for lifetimes.

To go into the core of who we are.

If we are afraid of our shadow, we're afraid of our own truth.

And where there is fear, there is no love.

The most courageous thing is to look at ALL of you, so you don't
project your shadow unconsciously.

When you KNOW that at your core that you are love, and that you
are loved—even when you witness the most painful, gruesome, dark,
shameful parts of yourself that have been trying to remain hidden—
you KNOW that it's time to hold more compassion, more love, and
more self-awareness than ever before.

From this place of your whole truth, you rise.

And what is more loving than truth?

The more I dive into my truth, the more I feel set free.

PURPOSE PROMPTS

What do you feel you are intuitively being guided to look at? Accept? Make peace with? Take responsibility for? Forgive? Know that you did the best you could with what you had and choose to love yourself fully. What are you ready to let go of, to hand over to the Universe to release a weight within? What parts of you can you love and accept even deeper than ever before?

If things come up through this process that you want to get off your chest, it can be helpful to write it all down and burn it or throw it away when you're done. Sometimes just writing things out helps to get them off our chest, allows that part of us that's been holding onto it to be heard, and gives us an opportunity to express what may be years, or decades of things we've never had the opportunity to express.

_____

_____

_____

_____

_____

_____

_____

_____

_____

_____

_____

I'M NO LONGER AFRAID OF THE DARK

As I dive into all depths of my being, I'm no longer afraid of the dark.

To hold forth in the coming times, it's important to be able to stand our ground with strength. With compassion.
With loving awareness.

This level of strength is only possible when we learn how to love ourselves fully and wholly.
This is only possible by standing in truth.

Light AND dark.
Illuminating the shadows by penetrating them with light.

Being present with what is in order to hold faith in what we are creating, and what is to come.

Day by day I dive deeper into the depths of my shadows. To love the darkness into light.

To hold my ugliest aspects with unconditional love.

To unhook from the shame-guilt trap we've collectively built our world on, keeping many light leaders unconsciously stuck in their own sabotaging cycles.

I, too, have caught myself in this trap... many times.

The journey to sovereignty and liberation as we co-create the new earth is not just of light codes and higher dimensional beings.

It's delving into the depths of our beings to unhook ourselves from millennia of darkness passed down to us ancestrally and collectively, and that which we hold in our soul-memory of other lifetimes here.

The density of this planet is a challenge for many healers, light workers, star seeds (you know, all the labels!). Many of us find ourselves battling addictions, mental health issues, and a gnawing desire to escape.

By awareness and understanding of how to walk WITH the density and darkness, we allow our light to shine brighter. It is only through our humanity that we can fully anchor 5D consciousness into the planet, and fully help others in their journey.

RELEASE CONTROL IN RELATIONSHIPS

When someone is not giving you what you want, or fulfilling your needs, regardless of the type of relationship, do not try to make them give you what you need.

Instead, see if you can give it to yourself.

Our desire to control another and "make them" give us "what we need" is a form of shadow, and a toxic habit to seek validation, love, or fulfilment from anyone external to us.

For example, if you're in a friendship and the other person isn't giving you what you need—whether it be attention, time, or your desired level of energy—rather than getting annoyed at them, ask yourself why you desire this from them?

The same goes for romantic relationships. If you are craving your partner's love in order to feel loved, validated, or loveable, you're placing your own worthiness and love-ability onto another person.

When you remember that YOU ARE LOVE, therefore YOU ARE LOVEABLE, and YOU ARE WORTHY, YOU ARE ENOUGH, YOU ARE WONDERFUL, YOU ARE A MAGNIFICENT BEING OF THE UNIVERSE... Then you stop giving away your power, and you stop operating from a place of trying to control another.

When you love yourself, remember your natural worthiness, feel whole and complete, and do not NEED the love of another, you begin to magnetize people who love you for the real you that you are, and treat you in the ways you desire and deserve—with love and respect. I've been in both situations, begging boyfriends and people to love me more, give me more attention, and validate me in order for me to feel what I so deeply craved... fulfilment of love.

And I've had friends beg me for more attention, time, and love.

And here's what I have learned.

When I was the one begging, I didn't feel love inside of me, and no matter how hard I tried to make people love me—demanding love from my boyfriends, convincing my friends to spend time with me, even if they didn't necessarily want to go out partying, (that was my only way of spending time with my friends back then)—I STILL felt empty. Even WHEN they had obliged and given me what I was supposedly asking for.

Eventually, boyfriends could not give me what I wanted, and they left. And girlfriends got sick of my party ways, and my relationships became one sided.

When I've had friends wanting more from me than I've been able to give, I notice the same pattern. If I gave more than I felt I could (depleting my own energy to satisfy theirs as the martyr), they STILL wouldn't be satisfied and still demanded more of me.

As I was re-learning how to fully love myself, I realized it was a dance of not controlling another human, and simultaneously not letting myself be controlled.

When we let ourselves be controlled by another, not only are we giving our power to them, but we aren't allowing them the opportunity to heal and learn to love themselves.

We are feeding their addiction. And simultaneously, when we beg for love from others, or want more from them than they are giving us, we are feeding our own shadow.

When I lovingly told friends in the past that I could not meet their needs as they were asking, they've left the relationship usually hurt and upset and feeling rejected. The people pleaser in me wants to take my words back and give them what they want again.

However, like a child who wants candy for dinner, a loving parent would decline, as upset as the child might become. And while these are never parent-child relationships, as loving humans, whatever we feed persists.

Boundaries and self-love are vital ingredients in creating our wealthiest, happiest life.

And the way to happiness is to face the darkness.

When I discovered my own pattern of begging others for love and attention, and then being so hurt when this ended up pushing them away, I realized I had to become my own best friend.

I called it "dating myself."

Now, we are still human beings who are all interconnected with one another.

We are still going to want to be loved by others.

We are still going to want to spend time with people and have the energy and attention of our loved ones.

However, the secret to happiness in relationships is inter- dependence, not co-dependence.

When you love yourself so much, so wholly and completely (healing and forgiving all shame, guilt, remorse, blame, and victim consciousness within us, which usually creates our ego-shadow that needs to be fed through control and manipulation in the first place), you get to bring YOUR BEST SELF to all relationships, starting with the one with yourself.

You get to enter empowered, loving relationships. Where control and manipulation are a thing of the past, and the relationship is one of two individuals who CHOOSE to accompany each other through the joys of life.

When you stop trying to control others, and allowing yourself to be controlled, you reclaim your boundaries, your sovereignty, and you CHOOSE who and how to love.

When you remove obligation from relationships, you remove fear. And when you remove fear, you are met with its opposite, love.

Love breeds love.

When you love yourself, and don't NEED another human being to fulfil your needs, when you learn how to fulfil your needs from within, you get to show up in all areas of life loved, loving, loveable, and complete.

When you're vibrating at a frequency of LOVE... guess what you attract more of?!

That's right. Love breeds love.

And there are no exceptions to that rule.

PURPOSE PROMPTS

What do you desire in your relationships? Consider all relationships in your life—friendships, intimate partnerships, romantic relationships, working or business relationships.

_____

_____

_____

_____

_____

_____

_____

How do you desire to feel in your relationships? How do you desire to be treated?

_____

_____

_____

_____

_____

What sort of friend, partner, family member, or business partner do you desire to be?

_____

_____

_____

_____

_____

How similar is this to how you are now in relationships?

_____

_____

_____

_____

_____

Seeing this as an opportunity to become the person you desire to be (and absolutely no judgments or beating yourself up in this process!) what changes—if any—are you being intuitively guided to make?

_____

_____

_____

_____

_____

_____

DIVING INTO THE DARKNESS

TO BE HUMAN IS TO FEEL. TO EXPERIENCE.

This doesn't mean to project onto another. When we learn to experience our emotions, our feelings, as simply an experience, as real as they might seem, we allow ourselves to heal. I can't explain the darkness. But I can give you an insight into healing it, without harming myself or another anymore.

I am a fan of the light. I love it. For most of my life, I felt ashamed of my darkness. It had nowhere to go. I would suppress it, avoid it, numb it, hide it, and in all honesty, I'm not sure I ever consciously acknowledged it. It was a part of me I was so ashamed of. I had days of darkness and I did not share them with anyone. It went against everyone's perception of me, including my own. But when I was in my daily life and caught off guard, it would leak out when I least expected it, and I would projectile vomit this anger, rage, or self-loathing onto whomever was around—usually those closest to me, my family, or when I was wasted. I would do and say things, feeling so embarrassed afterwards. I would say awful things to my family and regret them afterwards once I'd calmed down or sobered up.

It is something I have been consciously working on for years, and the deepest work has been experiencing my own anger, rage, and deep emotion, without projecting it onto another. A by-product is that I no longer get angry and have a tantrum at the coffee table if I bump into it.

The only difference is that now, I know how to transmute it without energetically vomiting all over those around me (mostly my husband, who still calls me out when I'm trying to bring him into my own shit. We're both big on taking personal responsibility for our own emotions and energy. Trying to blame the other person or make ourselves the victim doesn't work in our relationship; we've consciously chosen a path of healing, self-love, and sovereignty. Anything else doesn't stand a chance. It's also the main reason we hardly ever argue. We both take responsibility for our own shit, and have strong boundaries in what we will and will not tolerate).

Now instead, I will take myself for a walk, do some breathwork, go to the gym, or for a run, get outside into nature, or if it's safer to stay at home (i.e., don't drive while angry, it's dangerous), I will do some boxing or movement or drumming or writing. I will let myself feel all the emotions, all the pain, and ask myself, or my inner child, what I need.

Anything to purge the energy out.

I wrote the below piece during a time of purging the darkness. I used all my tools and had given myself a shamanic healing. Nothing was shifting the density, so I chose to turn the energy into words. It feels so vulnerable to share. It's raw, yet a very real truth for many, that society shuns away from speaking about.

My intention in sharing this is to share with you parts of me I thought I always had to keep hidden.

I hope that by doing so, you, or someone else reading this, feels less alone in anything you might feel ashamed of.

It's time we all fully learn to love ourselves. Not just the pretty, easy-to-share parts, but the raw, real, and deep truths that collectively we all carry. No more sweeping our fullness under the rug. The only way we can fully love ourselves is by bringing awareness and light to all the places light is not, and where love is missing.

Only then, can we feel truly free. When we share our deeper truths and experiences, we create a space for deeper connection within ourselves, and within humanity.

RAW OF THE DARK

How many times can I let go of all the parts of me I know?

How much longer can I feel this pain

This darkness

This rage

This fierce

Wild

Untamed

Emotion

That won't be still

until I express it?

Let it all out.

Why do I hold so much rage?

So much anger?

So much untamed emotion?

How much of this density can I dive into?

How deep does it go?

As I journey into the depth of the earth

Feeling Gaia pull me to her core

And pull out of me all the holes

Where I see worms crawling,

I know this is not my truth.

I know I am light.

But this crawling emotion

Doesn't dissipate.

The darkness invites me deeper.

Is it wrong?

Why do I feel guilty for the dark?

Is it my dark?

Or am I simply exploring it, experiencing as part of this human experience

So I can penetrate each part of my being

And know the dark?

Know what tempts it, alluring me deeper into it.

As I type, instead of my usual meditation music, I feel the temptation of Rage Against The Machine.

Somehow in this moment

The very things I used to shy away from

Allow me a moment of relief.

A music that gets me.

Sound that speaks the rage I feel

That my tears dance to

My light cannot stand it

Yet my inner rebel froths at the very rebellion of such darkness.

Is it really possible to enjoy this?

Or is that simply the art of surrender?

I notice the more I let my rage out—not at anyone or anything, simply let it out—Gaia is pulling my weeds out of me. The grungy music almost exorcising my darkness out of me. I begin to feel a peace. A deeper wholeness.

Could it be possible then, that the more I surrender to my darkness, it no longer plagues the light, but loses its temptation to come out when I least expect it?
Why do I have so much anger?

Is it the knowing at what my ancestors have done to the land?

Is it having seen what humans do to each other, stored in the collective belief system?

Is it seeing more truth around human trafficking and pedophilia rings?

Is it anything to do with being used for my woman-body?

Is it anything to do with being hushed as a child, being told how to feel and what to think when my soul held a wisdom that couldn't be communicated from my human as a child?

The more I surrender to feeling it all, without judgment or self-loathing or projecting it onto another or harming anyone or anything, the more whole I feel.

The more I learn to love all of me.

BELIEVE ME WHEN I SAY

In my dark nights of soul, when I was recovering from my alcohol addiction; I wanted to quit and go buy twelve bottles of wine and make all the pain go away again.

I had an insight.

As I was there lying on the floor, drowning in the depth of my darkness and tears,

I heard: "I can either deal with this now, or have to deal with it after this life ends."

So what did I choose in that moment of misery?

Well, I'm now about to celebrate five years since my last drink.

Believe me when I say, miracles happen.

Keep going.

ONE DAY AT A TIME

So many of us desire to make a deeply positive impact in the world.

CHANGE THE WORLD. HEAL THE WORLD.

Our souls scream.

The only problem is, we can't truly heal and change the world until we first heal and change OUR world.

When you heal and change your world, you can heal and change THE world, in the way your soul was born to.

If we look at healing from a mind perspective, it can be a total mindfuck.

There's our inner child
Our emotions
Our thoughts
Our subconscious
Our mind
Our heart
Our soul
Our multi-dimensional self-existing in other dimensions
There is the eternal part of us
There is the oneness as we connect to all of the universe
and source
There is the illusion of separation in this human life
There are our past lives
Our ancestors
Our collective
Our planet
The land we live on
The community we were brought up in
Our mothers' wounds

Our fathers' wounds
Our ancestors' traumas
Empathic feeling of others' wounds
Energy flowing through our energy bodies
Our connection to the earth
Our connection to the cosmos
Our future selves
Our past selves
Different versions of us
Personalities
Ego
Who we want to be
Who we want to become
Who we were
Who we are no longer
There is the part of us that'll leave a legacy of sorts
There is the world before we existed
And after we cease to exist in this life
Our cosmic family
Our human family
Our guides and cosmic guidance
God
The Universe
Source energy
Stagnant energy in the land
The animals and plants and mother earth
And all the rest of it

And we can
Practice mindfulness
Align our chakras
Meditate
Be one with the universe
Love our neighbor
Know thyself
Sit in plant medicine ceremony
Practice yoga
Tai chi

Qi Gong
Exercise
Journal
Forgive
Practice gratitude
Process our emotions
Sit in circles
Work with medicine, Western or Eastern
Practice energy healing
Or shamanic journeying
Or ancient healing
There's massage
And reflexology
And Chinese medicine
And therapy
And counselling
And psychologists
And group therapy
There's recovery circles
And community groups
And support groups
Online and offline
There are plants and fruit and herbs and natural remedies
There are wellness centers
And doctors
And therapists
And wellness experts
And health
And wellbeing
And healing circles
And online courses
And tools
And crystals
Oils
Incense
Candles
Affirmations
We can learn to remote view or astral travel

Or receive or give clairvoyant readings
Connect with mediums and speak with the other side
We can sit in stillness
And practice BEing
And connect with the I AM part of us
We can lose our identities
And recreate our identities
We can question our identities
And decide on our identities
We can be multi-faceted
And choose labels
Or remove labels
We can do lots
Or do little
We can be still
Or avoid
Or be active and busy
We can honor our seasons
And rhythms
And cycles
Or we can ignore them and get lost in our own being
Get caught in the trap of the mind
We can know we are the awareness of our thoughts
Or become confused and listen to our thoughts as truth
We can change our vibrations
And choose a new frequency
And choose new thoughts
And process old thoughts
Release old behaviors
And habits
And patterns
And decide on a new way of being
And choose to be our best versions of self
And all the while asking "Who am I?!"
We can answer it in labels
Or titles
Or with more questions
We can come from a place of confidence

Or uncertainty
For what if we say we are one thing
But we are another?
What if we give ourselves the wrong title
Or there is no label for who we are?
"Does my name even fit me?"
Why this name?
Who would I be with a different name?
What would it be like if I changed my name or my title or my label?
How do I present to the world?
Who am I choosing to be?
Do I focus on myself?
Or do I give to others?
Or both?
And how?
Am I ready to give to others?
Can I listen to others deeply enough to help them change?
Do I even help them, or do I hold space and they help themselves?
What does it mean to be fully liberated?
What does it mean to be free?
Who am I?
What do I want?
What do I desire?
How could I possibly want more?
How can I love more when I'm struggling to love myself more?
How can I love myself more?
Do I really carry this much darkness, or is this the
collective entanglement?
Are these emotions mine, or am I empathetically feeling them?
I know it's up to me to release them... but do I even need to, or will
they disappear by themselves?
Is now the time to go within, or to hustle and achieve?

Except... healing isn't a mind thing.

Your higher self knows what you need. Your heart knows the
way. Your body holds a wisdom and intelligence created by The
Universe herself.

And so, start.

One day at a time. One breath at a time.

This too shall pass.

How can you love your way through today, a little more than yesterday?

How can you find more gratitude in today?

How can you be the best you, just for today?

And so, just for today, we change our lives.

One day at a time.

PURPOSE PROMPTS

Just for today, what are you most proud of yourself for?

_____

_____

_____

_____

_____

Each time you desire to rise.

Going deeper within first is imperative.

You can only grow as deep as you dig.

Like the oak tree that stands sturdy to withstand any storm.

To heal the world, you must first heal yourself.

From a shamanic perspective,

Look at the world from an energetic vantage point.

There is a web of energy. These energies can be belief patterns, soul contracts, and agreements. Some are positive, healthy, and connected to love frequencies. When people are connected to them, they're tapped into source energy and are able to listen to their OWN intuitive guidance more easily... the messages directly for them (not another human).

Some, on the other hand, are lower vibration and fear-based. Society, for the most part, is based on this energetic entanglement of fear-based belief systems. Where instead of each person trusting themselves, they look to their leaders or other people outside their own family or inner circle of trust... they look to people who don't always have the best intentions for them.

We see this on a global scale with governments and "matrix" systems that have unconsciously enslaved humanity over time.

We're now at a time of collective liberation, awakening, and global freedom.

This process will probably feel messy. When people realize who they truly are, and see through illusions of what they've been led to believe or base their entire lives upon, it can lead to chaos, inner disruption, confusion, shame, guilt, resentment, anger, and frustration.

This is natural, and to be expected.

The journey to love, when one has been doused unconsciously in fear masquerading as love, can feel dark, lonely, and confusing.

One day at a time.

Start with one breath, one word in your journal, one song to begin shaking the energy off.

There's no rush.

Just be compassionate towards yourself.

And begin to observe your cyclical nature.

And so, just for today, we change our lives.

One day at a time.

Right now, I'm coming out of a "winter" phase of my life. Perhaps you are, too.

Just like the seasons of the planet, we too have seasons as humans.

We have seasons in a day, a week, a month, and a year, perhaps even a decade.

In spring, new seeds are sprouting, new growth is happening, hope is on the horizon.

Summer brings bountiful abundance, energy, opportunity, and much promise.

Autumn is a time for harvesting, giving thanks, reaping rewards, and reflection.

Winter is a time for rest, rejuvenation, shedding, releasing, and letting go of the old, knowing Spring is near.

Many people experience bouts of depression or sadness in winter. I've been here many times.

When I resist it and want to be in my personal "summer" when my natural rhythm is in "winter," I feel anxious, depressed, and frustrated.

However, when I surrender to it being a time for within-ness and relinquish control, I begin to enjoy it and love myself through the process. In saying that, if you—like me—are highly tapped into energy and feel what others are feeling, either around you, or in the collective... during a "winter" time, if you're not taking care of your own needs and trying to give to others without giving to yourself, you're going to find yourself carrying the weight of the world on your shoulders.

You may feel tired, drained, lethargic, irritable, or sad for no reason.

You might feel the density of the planet as a whole. I know for myself, and many people I work with, whenever there are heavy things happening in the world, we feel it.

The more you ground into your own journey, look within through meditating and journaling, and learn to listen to your own intuitive guidance, opening your direct connection and relationship with the Universe / God / Source / Creator and allowing any external energy to bounce off your own energy field, you'll be able to hold your pillar of light as an anchor in the energetic or collective chaos happening around you.

As you go through your own healing and self-love journey, unhooking from collective shadows through your own healing and removing frequencies of resonance with things going on collectively, you'll be able to observe the world around you and hold your pillar of light from a place of compassion and strength rather than getting caught in any collective waves... truly being able to assist others, without getting caught in their energetic and emotional tsunamis.

PURPOSE PROMPTS

What does ultimate self-care, self-love, and nourishment look like to you? What makes you feel really good? Is it taking 15 minutes to meditate or journal before you start your day? Is it choosing more nourishing foods to fuel your body? Is it turning off your phone at night? Is it all of these and more? The more you take care of you, the easier you'll be able to take care of others.

_____

_____

_____

_____

_____

What changes get to happen to include more you time, to look after yourself and upgrade your self-care and self-love to support you in your deepest happiness?

_____

_____

_____

_____

_____

YOU ARE A MIRACLE

You're here today and have overcome so much
Things that were scary, things that took
incredible courage
Perhaps even things that nearly killed you

You've had your heart broken, probably numerous times
You've been unfairly treated, probably numerous times
You've been so sad you didn't know
how you'd get through it
And you did!
Probably numerous times

Perhaps you're going through one of
these times at the moment
Perhaps you've just come out of one of these times
And you know what
The way that every time life happens
Because life always happens
And you respond, react, surrender, accept,
grieve, forgive, cry, learn, and grow
And every other beautiful emotion
you have up your sleeve
Using all the tools you have
And then bounce back
Is absolutely amazing

Resilient, strong, powerful, beautiful, brave
Beyond comprehension
The way you allow these things to flow through
you in the way only you know how
Is a miracle

You have a decision to make:
To grow, learn, and be stronger than before
Or to let it consume you and become life's victim

But I know you
Nothing is getting in your way.

You take all of life's challenges, feel them, breathe
them in
Pain and all
And you add them to your tool-belt of strength

You're a warrior
A creator
A divine human being
You're a Miracle
That's what you are
You're amazing, I am in awe of you
Many others are in awe of you too
The things you rise above
The obstacles you use as steppingstones!
You are life
You are love
You are a Miracle

FORGIVENESS

To all men and women who have ever been raped, sexually abused, or harassed:

I see you.

I am you.

At this time of collective awakening, we are being asked to go deeper into our healing.

Far too many women, and men, have experienced some form of sexual abuse.

It's no coincidence we're going deeper into these journeys at this time, as we begin to remember our divine femininity, as individuals, and as a collective.

Many of us have blocked our very ability to BE and RECEIVE, to avoid receiving unwanted advances—physical or not.

We're coming out of an age of darkness, and in order to hold more light, we go back into our own darkness to heal.

Deep forgiveness work and energetic trauma releasing is vital.
Even if we've spent years doing this, we're being called to go deeper, peel back more layers, to be able to hold more light.

Where there is light, there is love.
Where there is love, there is no fear.
Where there is no fear, we radiate more love.
In order for the goddess to rise as we create alignment within humanity and the planet, it is important to remember to choose love.
I see a world where it is possible to forgive our abusers and hold compassion for our perpetrators. To fully heal and let the pain crack us wide open as we learn to love ourselves again.
I see a world where every human sees one another as equals, regardless of gender, sex, race, or religion.

But how do we heal humanity? By starting with ourselves.

I remember a ceremony I sat in Bali where I was doing ancient ritual work and uncovered new layers I had been hiding from myself in shame and not-enoughness.

Shame of being a woman. Shame of my female body, of my cycles and of the full expression of my nature.

Where this shame had come from is not as important as the awareness and healing OF these deeper layers stored in my being.

It's a belief stored deeply in our collective belief systems that most of us are born into.
Women, men, and all genders have been raised in this system, with porn for education, and ancestral memory of violence and abuse in our collective DNA.

As we embody more of our truth, by healing all that is NOT our truth, we do so for future generations, past generations, and the collective as a whole.

At this time, we are remembering the magnificence of our inner goddess, our divine feminine—as all genders, across all of humanity.

We embody grace, kindness, and a gentle nurturing of all things, balanced with the strength of a warrior and heart of a lion.

My energy practices became far more intentional and deeper as I committed each day to the sacred journey of a magnificent abundant life, in the knowing that it is through the ripple effect of our collective efforts that humanity will change forever.

Together we heal. Together we rise. Together we activate remembrance of our full power and activate the codes and embodiment of heaven on earth once again.

THE ONLY WAY TO HEAL IS TO FEEL

I have heard people saying that talking about love and light when it comes to our traumas is spiritual bypassing.

I like to see forgiveness as the last layer of healing of a particular event or energy we have experienced and are letting go of.
Some things require more focus on forgiving and having compassion than others, but none of it is bypassing what was.

When we experience trauma, pain, or abuse in our pasts, regardless of where it has come from, it is our job to heal from it.

This does not mean ignoring it and trying to replace it with love and light.

Quite the opposite.

It means facing the very thing we've often spent years ignoring, suppressing, or trying to escape from.

I was 14 when I was raped.

I never told anyone what truly happened, laughing much of it off with friends. I absorbed bullying about it and carried the shame of it, for years.

I began to use alcohol problematically and escaped from my physical reality in any way I could. I developed eating disorders and tried to end my life on several occasions as I could not bear to be alone with myself.

When I finally stopped drinking, I had to get to know myself again.

I had to learn how to have conversations sober when I was out socializing. I became a hermit for months and watched Netflix when I realized human interacting was harder than I thought when my main crux of identity had been ripped apart.

I'd been hiding behind it for all of my later teens and my entire twenties up until that point.

I'd been going to these "spiritual circles" for a few months before my rock bottom event.

I reached out to the teacher, and asked her for a clairvoyant reading.

I'd never had one before; I was always taught they were evil and the work of the devil, having been brought up in a Christian family.

I was so nervous before our call.

When I received the reading and explained that I wanted direction and clarity and explained my situation, being newly sober and having no fucking clue what I was doing,

She said, "Let's have a look at why you were drinking in the first place."

During the reading, two profound things came up.

Firstly, she said, "There was some sort of sexual interference."

Right then, I knew exactly what it was.

The second thing she brought up that had me with tears of grace running down my face, feeling more seen, supported, and held than perhaps ever before, was, "Dane's dad is here, he is so proud of you and is supporting you in this."

I'd never met Dane's dad.

He died from liver failure after a lifetime as an alcoholic when Dane was 16.

I began to connect the dots.

This was so much bigger than I could see. I am so supported. I am so guided. I am so loved.

After discovering the sexual trauma I was carrying, I booked another session to go deeper into my healing.

She guided me through my first ever soul regression, or inner child healing where I went back and visited that version of me that had just been raped.

I loved her and held her and gave her the emotional support she needed in that moment.

The months and years following that were the darkest shadow processing. Seeing, reliving, and finally allowing myself to process the emotions that I never expressed in that moment.
Oh, there was so much anger, hatred, frustration—my innocence ripped away that I would never get back.

I felt it all.

I realized the only way to heal is to feel.

That became my mantra when I was crying myself to sleep or avoiding sleep because I didn't want to be alone with myself.

The only way to heal is to feel.

The only way to heal is to feel.

Where that mantra had come from, I don't know. But it saved me. It saved my life, and I knew it was the touch of grace.

I would actively go to healing circles and go to the beach to scream, punch pillows, stomp out my anger, and punch the air in anger. Anger of my innocence being taken away was the most common one.

I came to a point where I was ready to forgive.
Oh my goddess, that was a big one.
I forgave, and I forgave, and I forgave.

I held compassion for my abuser.

I forgave some more, until I could only feel love in my body.

I feel like I have completely forgiven, but the thing with our healing journeys is they aren't linear.

Sometimes I think I've worked on something, and I find myself in a situation, realizing there's more layers of that one thing.

For me, my goal is love.

That is my intention behind all I do and all I am.
I am human and I am learning to love.

It is a process.

So when you hear someone talking about forgiveness and love, feel what that means for you.

Understand the process is deep, sometimes incredibly dark, and it's through the cracks in our darkness that light shines through.

I FORGIVE YOU

I forgive you.

I forgive you for spending your teenage years and half of your twenties drunk.

I forgive you for putting all your energy into drinking and getting messed up.

I forgive you for putting your self-worth on being the life of the party, and how much attention you received from men.

I forgive you for not respecting your body.

I forgive you for the toxins you fuelled yourself with.

I forgive you for your unreliability.

I forgive you for your mistakes.

I'm sorry you felt you had to be so strong.

I forgive you for not asking for help.

I forgive you for protecting yourself in the only way you knew how.
I forgive you for all the people you hurt.

I forgive you.

I thank you.

I thank you for the strength you've provided me.

I thank you for teaching me resilience.

I thank you for showing me my need for fun.

I thank you for the mistakes.

I thank you for showing me the importance of being grounded.

Opposites teach us big things, don't they?

I thank you for the many, many life lessons, at such a young age.

I thank you for the depth I now have. I would not have the capacity to
hold space for others as I now do, if it weren't for you, so I am deeply
grateful for you and all that you did for us.

I thank you for all you did for me.

For us.

I forgive you and I thank you.

What do you forgive yourself for?

MAKING PEACE WITH THE PAST

"God grant me the serenity to accept the things I cannot change, the courage to change the things I can, and the wisdom to know the difference"

--- Serenity Prayer

We are here on this planet to evolve. To experience all that it is to be human. For the evolution of humanity, and for the evolution of our souls.

We make mistakes.

It is okay.

It is okay to learn to love the version of you that made mistakes.

Truly.

The more love you have for yourself, the more love you hold on a vibrational level.

When you embody the frequency of love, of self-love, fully and completely, you'll begin to magnetize things into your life on that frequency.

You might have heard of the Law of Attraction?
This is how it works.

Notice.

The more you learn to love yourself, even the parts you have no clue how.

Through forgiveness, through learning the lessons you learned in those situations, and taking them with you into who you choose to be from this moment on.

And you remember, you are not bound to the past.

Nor are you bound to the future. All you have is now.

And when now you choose to be a better version of yourself, who chooses to forgive versions of you in the past, you'll pave the way to a much more loving, beautiful, abundant future.

Your world doesn't change from the outside.

It changes from within.

You hold the keys to unlock your dreams.
By choosing to love, forgive, and just for now, choosing who you will be, how you will love, and how you will let go of all that is keeping you stuck in the past.

YOU DID THE BEST WITH WHAT YOU HAD

When healing guilt

and shame

Remember

You did the best with

what you had.

You'll do better now.

Forgive yourself

Release it

Love yourself

PURPOSE PROMPTS

Write a letter of forgiveness to anyone you feel ready to forgive, that you're ready to release resentment around.

Write a letter of forgiveness to yourself, especially anything you are carrying guilt and shame around. It can be helpful to finish this letter with the gifts you received from this healing and letting go, and anything you are grateful to this version of you for.

FORGIVENESS TECHNIQUE

I forgive: _____ for _____. I hand this to the Universe and replace it with love.

Feel the piece you are forgiving leave your body and be replaced with love.

It can be helpful to say this out loud and repeat as often and as many times as needed.

JUDGMENTS

I used to make fun of people like me.

I probably used to make fun of people like you, too. I apologize. I would not have meant it personally.

I was ignorant and naive. That's no excuse, I know.

Please forgive me.

It helps me to not mind when people make fun of me now. I don't know why anyone would, but it's none of my business. (And I now love myself so deeply that I don't mind if people who don't vibe with me do not). People make fun of people when they don't understand them. I didn't understand people like me, so I made fun of them.

Why would anyone want to heal their past, fall in love with themselves, and live their best life, in total alignment with their absolute purpose?

Dunno.

Why would people want to discover their potential and find out what it means to be utterly fucking content with life?

Beats me.

Who the eff would put their health first and overcome anxiety and depression and heal the root causes of their multiple addictions?!

What the actual eff.

Who would want to wake up every morning grateful AF for just being alive?!? And then talk about how grateful they are for everything?! Weirdos.

Who would DO that?

I would. I do!

I used to laugh at people like me because it brought out insecurities. Now, I help people like I was to heal and overcome those insecurities.

STICK AT IT

I've done a few trips overseas and vacations since I've been sober, but as I hopped off the plane yesterday in Bali, the smell of incense brought me straight into the awareness I was in Asia, and memories flooded my mind of hungover day tours, drunken obnoxiousness, focusing on nothing but the Bintangs and whatever the local beer was, wherever I was.

Anyone who has ever travelled with me will remember that "beer o'clock" was anytime, anywhere, and with anyone.

Anyone who has ever travelled with me will also remember the destruction Drunk Libby would leave in her path. I apologize for that.

As I return this time with purpose, vision, clarity, and the best outlook on life, travel is no longer about the beers and bars, hangovers and laziness, but about connection, observation, nature, sun, and a continuation of creating MAGIC, all day every day!

Grateful, appreciative, and filled with joy doesn't even explain HALF of what life can be when you clean your shit up and turn your life around and stick at it.

That's the part most people forget.

Stick at it.

Literally, take things one day at a time. One moment at a time, trying to be the best version of yourself.

Just for today.

That's all it takes to create your dream life.

One day at a time.

A PRAYER FOR INNER PEACE FROM THE PAST

Place a hand on your heart as you read aloud or feel these words as you read in your mind.

I surrender to the truth

I hold space in my heart for the deepest love to penetrate through my body

I release all shame, all guilt, and all doubt of reclaiming who I am

I honor my truth and have clear boundaries with all else

I am free

Liberated

The constraints of my mind no longer taking control

The expectations of my surroundings and past no longer the ruling force

To step into my full power is to honor source and proceed with love

I'm done holding back

It's time to break free

No more boxes

No more restrictions

I forgive myself

Fully and wholly

Unlimited love

And so it is

TO THE LOVED ONES

It's pretty challenging watching someone you love suffer.

From the outside, it's easy to see a way out. The only problem is, the only true way out doesn't come from anyone or anything outside. It's gotta come from within. And when you're in it, it's all you know. Knowing there are people out there who love you, no matter what, no matter how bad you fucked up, definitely helps.

Addiction looks like:

Having an argument with your partner because of your drinking, swearing you'll never drink again, then finding yourself out 'til 5a.m., shoe-less, just one week later. Drinking before the pre-drinking before the pre drinks. Party, sleep, food, sleep, party, no money left, put it all on credit, party some more. Getting angry just at the thought of having to drive sober. Watching how quickly others around you are drinking and wishing they'd hurry up, so you could get your next drink without the guilt. Wondering where you are and what happened the night before. Finding any reason, time or place for a drink... "7am on a London Tube is a great time to have a cider—I'm about to do a nine-hour bike ride!"

These vignettes, if taken by themselves, may seem funny. But when addiction controls your entire life and you don't know how to stop, then it is a problem. I know, I did all these things. I wanted to stop and knew I had to. I just had no idea HOW. But I knew I had better figure it out—or it would be figured out for me.

Here's what I did after my last night of drinking and realizing I'd hit the last rock bottom I ever wanted to hit.

I said, "I have a problem. I need help. I can never drink again. Universe, HELP. I need your help more than ever. I'm doing this, I'm really doing this. Oh shit, what have I got myself in for." I didn't wanna be sober. It sounded dumb and lame as fuck.

I wasn't dumb or lame as fuck. I was me, Libby, who loved to party. Beers in the sun. Tequila. Shots, shots, shots. What's the time? Wine-o-clock.

But I was also not half the person I knew I could be.

And so, one day at a time, meditation, a spiritual awakening, many, MANY tears, anger and frustration, I fumbled my way through life, "dating myself," figuring out who I was beneath the layers of sav, cider, and any other numbing agent I could get my hands on.

Figuring out why I was even numbing in the first place.

Here's a tip and it's kinda hard to swallow; no one else can make the changes.

It's gotta come completely from within.

And in order to change, you gotta first admit that you messed up and need help.

Believe me, that's the hardest part.

The rest follows. Lose the ego, the heart will lead.

A LETTER TO THE LOVED ONES

And so, to all the friends, families, partners, and loved ones who witness their daughter, son, friend, spouse, sister, or brother go through addiction,

My heart goes to you.

It must be so hard witnessing someone putting themselves through pain and seeing from the outside what seems to be an out-of-control downward tornado.

Yes, this may seem a little heavy. So are the hearts of loved ones to someone in the midst of self-destructive addiction.

On behalf of my past self and anyone else who allows me, I am sorry. I am sorry for putting you through all I put you through. I'm sorry for putting you through torment, stress, and worry. I'm sorry for hurting you. I'm sorry for abusing you. I'm sorry for being so selfish. I'm sorry for continuously making the same mistakes, time and time again.

I am sorry.

Please feel my apology and know the entirety of its sincerity.

The best thing you can do as a loved one is loving your loved one and speaking up with love when you feel it's necessary. Set and speak your boundaries, too.

The most powerful question I got asked after my last night of yet another dangerously toxic escapade, this time miraculously surviving the drunken attempted suicide, was "What are you going to do about it?"

That question empowered me to realize that THIS, this behavior, this pain, was hurting too many others, including myself, and I couldn't run from it any longer.

In that moment, lying there at rock bottom, this question transformed my life.

From the ground up, I built my own revolution.

Yet as much as I have forgiven and let go, a piece of my heart will always feel the pain of loved ones of alcoholics, drug addicts, and those who live in patterns of destruction. My heart feels heavy with this pain. Speak about your pain. Let your loved one in turn speak about theirs.

After all, all addiction arises from a lack of love somewhere within our consciousness.

With all the love in my heart, I honor you, I love you.

Together we heal. Together we rise.

BE FUCKING AMAZING

I see you.

I feel you.

I see your strength, masked by pain.

I feel your love, masked by sorrow.

I see your beauty, masked by a filter, I feel you.

Well, sweet soul. It's time to shine.

You're done with dulling.

You're done with trying to fit into the smallness of gossip, drama, worry and jealousy. You know it doesn't serve you, and you're right.

You have permission to SHINE.

You have permission to be fucking AMAZING.

IT'S NOT ALWAYS ABOUT YOU

Your world revolves around you, but THE world does not.

We are all individual beings, going about our individual lives, thinking about ourselves and our own lives.

Which is great. Think about yourself, focus on loving yourself. Focus on how YOU can make the world a better place. And, of course, you think about others. Of course, you think about making the world a better place. Of course, you're sending people love-bombs when you think about them.

But in reality, when we're dealing with other humans, nothing is ever as personal as it may seem.

We are all just characters in each other's movies.

You're the star of your own show, not someone else's.

So next time someone doesn't message you back when you'd like them to, or if they say something in a way you don't agree with or look at you or don't look at you in the way you'd like... it's got nothing to do with you.

How you respond, that's on you.

If you notice yourself feeling offended easily, or judging people, or feeling sorry for yourself, that's an indicator that it is time to learn how to love yourself more. To be okay whether someone compliments you or doesn't speak to you or says something unpleasant to you. It is time to remember how freaking amazing you are without another human telling you so. Yes, it's nice to receive compliments. Yes, it's nice to receive validation from others. Yes, it's nice. But it can be so nice that it becomes an addiction, and when we don't get our hit of external validation—whatever means we're waiting for it from—we end up doubting our own brilliance, worthiness, and enough-ness.

You, beautiful human, are here on this planet. You are an expression of the Universe. To doubt yourself is to doubt The Creator. There is nothing wrong with you. Nothing at all. When you can know that, feel that, and embody that with every cell of your being, you'll unlock a remembrance of your potential, experience the beauty of life, step into new levels of success, AND make the world a better place just by being you.

We've created a world of illusion that we have to DO things in order to be worthy of love.

Beautiful soul, when you realize your mere existence on this planet is your permission slip to be worthy of love, without you needing to DO anything, you'll create a life of magic.

Beautiful soul. If you could see your heart, your potential, your power, your magnificence, your curiosity, your playfulness, your love, your unique quirks and traits you've tried to keep hidden your whole life, oh my goddess, would your world change.

You believed the bullies at school when they made fun of you for your laugh or your playfulness or your intellect. You thought it was about you.

You believed the adults around you as a child telling you "don't do that", or "be quiet," or "don't talk about that," or, "that's not acceptable." You thought it was about you.

You believed the magazines telling you what you need in order to be sexier, more beautiful, or to make a man love you. You thought it was about you.

You believed the insults thrown at you, or that mistakes were bad. You learned not to ask questions, or to speak up in case you were wrong. You believed your sensuality was a sin, and your love for life was weird.

Sweet soul, NONE of that was about you.

None of it.

It was all about the perspective from those who placed those dreamings, those scripts, on you. You were just a character in their movies.

It is time to rewrite the script. Hire a new director. Finally become the star of your own show.

You write the rules. The only person you report to is The Creator, and you realize what any of the characters in your show are or aren't doing is simply because they are in their own movie, their own show, their own reality, their own world.

When we can take responsibility for our own lives, love ourselves with or without another's permission to do so, and be the fullest expression of ourselves, the ripple effect will occur, and we'll create permission for those around us to do the same.

Laugh at your own jokes. Dance when you feel like it. Clap and cheer for the band in the quiet restaurant. Compliment the stranger. Smile at the homeless. Say thank you when someone lets you walk in the door first. Tip the waiter without them knowing and see their face as you walk away. Donate to a charity and don't tell anyone. Make memories without posting on socials. Touch your body with love. Feel your own touch. Feel the energy running from your hands as you place a hand on your heart. Feel the connection from your heart to the Universe. Bless your food when you're dining with friends. Look at yourself in the mirror—truly connect with yourself, your eyes, your soul. BREATHE. Take all of you in. See that?! Feel that?! YOU, sweet soul, are a work of art.

A one of a kind. A sacred being that no one and nothing can replicate. When you can give yourself the love you've been craving from the world, you'll realize that no one else's actions or behaviors were ever about you all along.

And as you remember this, and learn how to remove all need for attention, for validation, you'll find the type of freedom you've been searching for your whole life.

HEALING MEDITATION

I am source energy.
I am spirit in body.
To judge another is to judge yourself.
To judge yourself is to judge the divine.
To judge the divine is to doubt creation.
To doubt creation is insanity.
Love is the only way forward.
Acceptance, grace, compassion.

It must be clear to you, release all that does not serve you.
The pull of low energies holds you back. Release and let go immediately.

You are a work of art. An angel.
Remember that. We love you.
Allow us to guide you.
Not your fears, not low energies, not even your so-called enemies.
Do not judge. Simply say, "this is not for me."
And let it go.

This is the kindest thing you can do. Do not place your energy where it is wasted. Your time is precious. Your energy is precious.

Stop doubting.
Guide and be guided.
Love and be loved. Free and be freed.

New timelines and new energies are at work within and around you. The forces that guide you are closer than ever.
Listen. Trust. Listen to no one but your source.
Not even your doubting mind.
You think you're so alone. You're not.

Focus on your mission. Stop worrying about time. There is plenty. Look how far you've come!

Reflect! You're ascending rapidly, sometimes your body may need to catch up. Ensure you nourish yourself effectively. This will help. Have courage, we are with you each step of the way.

Release your doubts. Stop focusing on your environment, focus on your mission, you are doing so well. Keep going, we are with you, we love you.

SHAMANIC HEALING

One of the things I'm most grateful for about those few years living in Bali was the normalization of spirituality, of healing, of the ancient ways of being at one with each other and the Universe. A few months before we left, I sat in ceremony with a dear sister to go deeper into my own healing.

Along with my ancestors, guides, Papatuanuku, Earth Mother, and Ranginui, Father Sky, and sacred beings of this planet working with us as medicine in our healing journeys, my friend—a powerful healer—held me deep in a shamanic journey to go to some of the deepest parts of my being, pieces that felt unsafe to be here in this planet; pieces I've been carrying for a long time, energetically fighting each day.

I purged out old energy, feeling emotional and energetic traumas and wounds physically leaving my body. I met my warrior spirit, so strong, here to help the healing of humanity.

I was reminded that the true strength of a warrior, comes from grace.

A strength so pure, so beautiful… it's magnetizing.

The essence of warrior spirit dancing with dark and light to show true strength and bring deep healing through surrender and compassion.

Meeting the darkness with love and lovingly letting it go, thanking it for serving me while it did.

To be seen so vulnerably took huge courage.

I continue to heal and do deep work so I can continue to help heal the web of life and assist humanity in our ascension process.

So I can walk this planet the embodiment of my truth, and help others do the same.

So I can continue to rise and grow into all that I AM and all that I am here to BE.

For we can only grow as deep as we dig.

Together we heal, together we rise, together we co-create the new Earth.

SHEDDING THE PAST TO STEP INTO OUR FUTURE

The shedding process is one of deep surrender. To choose to let go of beliefs, habits, patterns that are no longer serving you, letting go of the only identity you've ever known and entering the void of the unknown can be one of the most frightening, exhilarating, and faith-provoking times we encounter.

Most of us expect to be able to answer the question when asked "WHO ARE YOU?" but in reality, most of us cannot. Not truly, until we've fully let go of all constructs we've been carrying that are, in fact, other people's perceptions, beliefs, and opinions OF us.

Only then, when we truly give ourselves permission to let go of all that we've ever known, can we truly discover, learn, and see not just who we are, but who we have come here to be.

If you're shedding layers of the "old you" like never before and preparing to step into the next level of yourself, you may have been noticing old emotions, patterns, anxieties, and doubts coming up to surface.

The art of shifting through them is not to ignore them or wish they weren't there... but to process them while learning the difference between thought and emotion.

If your thoughts aren't serving you, choose new thoughts (this can be way easier said than done, I know, I get it... it's a practice). However, do not try to push your emotions away, as that makes them stronger. If you're feeling anxious, ask why, perhaps process the emotion in the way it wants to be processed (cry, exercise, journal, talk to someone, watch an inspiring movie, be in nature, sleep, rest, etc.)

The more you're able to tune into your body and listen to what it's saying, the easier it becomes to listen to your heart and what it's whispering to you (this is probably what I love most about being sober; I was so disconnected from my body when I was numbing out and drinking all the time).

With each new level we step into, everything below the surface that has been getting in the way of us embodying that next level comes up for us to work through so we can step into higher alignment WITH that new level and clear out the old to learn lessons for the new.

LEARN THE LESSON SO YOU CAN MOVE ON:

If you keep finding yourself in the same situations, the same dramas, the same things repeating themselves, even if there are different people, different places, and different circumstances involved, it's because you haven't learned the lesson necessary for your soul evolution.

Ask yourself:

What lesson am I learning?

How is this situation helping me grow?

What sort of person am I choosing to be?

How am I choosing to handle this?

This requires an amount of humility, heart, and radical personal responsibility.

No amount of blame or placing ourselves as victims will make our lives change.

Things will repeat until we close the circle by learning and implementing the lesson.

Each time the same type of situation occurs is either to show you how much you've grown internally, or the lessons still yet to be learned. Learn how to do this and you'll create leaps in your journey to success.

THE MAGIC IS REAL

When we learn from Mother Earth and all beings living here, from plants, forests, waterways, the elements, and all creatures who inhabit her, we learn more about ourselves.

The last few months, I have been working with the energy of the Snake in my Shamanic journeys.

Snakes are vastly misunderstood creatures (relatable!). They are incredibly connected to the land and can help us with rooting and grounding to the earth. They show us the power of letting go of the old as they go through a natural death—rebirth cycle when they shed their skin.

We, too, go through a natural death—rebirth cycle, each day, if we allow ourselves to transform each day. Each time we go to sleep, we can set an intention to release all that no longer serves us and wake tomorrow anew.

I work with this energy to help me energetically shed old ancestral and collective beliefs, especially around fear, victimhood, and poverty consciousness. I used to be afraid of snakes, both physically, and from what I learned, biblically.

Part of my shamanic journey has been surrendering to more and more love, for all of life, for all of the planet, for all of the cosmos, each and every day.

First, I learned to energetically be okay with them and work with the spirit of snake through shamanic journey work. Then I began to see more of them here in Bali, lots on our driveway as I was coming or leaving my villa on the scooter.

I loved the shifts I have when I work with them in Shamanic journeying. I then gifted myself a snake necklace for my birthday to remind me of the beauty of this creature. Then I thought to myself, "All I need to do now is to hold one in real life." And, of course, a few days later, what do I see on the beach? None other than a woman walking with her pet snake wrapped around her shoulders.

She walked right up to us and started talking to us... then I got to hold her! A Boa Constrictor... cousin to the Anaconda.
Her name was Victoria.

PURPOSE PROMPTS

What has mother Earth taught you recently?

_____

_____

_____

_____

_____

_____

Next time you are out in nature, connect with an animal, a tree, water, land, a mountain or rock, and ask "What am I able to learn?" Observe the wisdom that follows.

YOU ARE THE REVOLUTION

Be so fucking committed to your growth and mission that your external world has no option but to match that.

When you hold the vibration of UTTER COMMITMENT

to your vision

to the Earth you are co-creating

to the life you are stepping into

to the impact you are making

to the revolutionary changes you KNOW are possible for humanity

and you surrender to thinking you have to do it alone,

and you let the Universe guide you

and you hang up your worries of judgment and fears of rejection

and you remember your magnificence, resilience, and power

And do what it takes to SHOW UP

Each day

And shed layers. Honoring the cosmic death, rebirth, death, rebirth, death, rebirth of generational and collective entanglements you'd found yourself in

And you have the courageous conversations

And honor your knowing over that of everyone else who thinks they know what's best for you

Do the work.
Have the faith.

And see miracle upon miracle upon miracle unfold right before your eyes.

You ARE magic.

You ARE a magnet for miracles.

You ARE here to be part of the REVOLUTION.

You ARE the revolution.

Stop hiding. Stop waiting. Take action now. There are too many people suffering, struggling, and needing your courage to rise, to lead your movement, to make changes in your life, family, business, and community.

Be so fucking committed that it literally becomes IMPOSSIBLE for the Universe not to match your desires.

Be the change.
Commit to it.
Each and every day.

THE SUPPORT OF OUR ANCESTORS

I've always been fascinated with the reasons we are here, what we're doing, and why.

Shamanism has always intrigued me, even if it probably used to freak me out a bit. But in all honesty, it has helped me answer, or at least find comfort in, so many questions I ask about the meaning, purpose, and mysteries of life and the Universe.

I realized I was studying shamanism before I even knew what it was.

I love knowing the protection, guidance, and incredible support we have from our ancestors and guides in spirit (if we are willing to be available to listen and receive it, often many of us are waiting for support, but we forget to ask!).

In one of my first shamanic meditations, I connected with the ancestors helping me. They had an indigenous energy and were there to help me embody ancient practices and wisdom through natural healing and to combine shamanism with business for progressive leadership in the world you and I are consciously creating, or at least, wanting to create! The importance of humanity being in right relationship with the planet is paramount if we want our species to survive. Businesses can be a powerful way to create change in communities.

In my second journey, I was shown my maternal grandfather (who I called grandad) and my paternal grandmother (Nana Mac). They are helping me to heal addictions and diseases in my ancestral line, as well as aggressive, abusive, controlling, and manipulative behaviors, especially in marriage and relationships. Dane and I are both consciously healing non-serving behaviors so that we break generational patterns.

Also here to teach me is my inner child. She reminds me about play, freedom, joy, happiness, more play, and also being in the moment, exactly as it is.

In my third journey connecting to spirits helping me, I was shown my unborn children, re-incarnating. They're here to heal, protect, and bring light into the world. Their energy is playful and fun, which is one of the reasons they've chosen Dane and me as parents. When I connected with their souls, I was shown how I am going to teach them much about their intuitive gifts, healing and magic, and play and entrepreneurship. In this journey, I was only shown what I teach them, not what Dane is teaching them. I'm so excited to meet them and learn from them, and so grateful for these tools and techniques to access the spiritual realms for further guidance in life.

PURPOSE PROMPTS

Call upon the support of your benevolent ancestors for any obstacle you may be facing, or any new project you may be birthing.

Simply say, "I call upon the support of Source and my benevolent ancestors to guide me to the highest outcome for all, thank you."

PART FIVE: REMEMBERING SOVEREIGNTY AND FREEDOM

OPENING UP TO MY SPIRITUALITY

I used to be terrified of readings, clairvoyants, mediums and anything "new age" or "spiritual."

I would never get a reading because I thought they were evil and scary, and I was afraid I would receive evil and scary news.

When I started realizing that spirituality was my jam, it made science and religion walk together instead of opposing one another (I was brought up religious and liked the "love and peace" part, yet I didn't like all the rules, and I completed a bachelor of science, so they seemed so opposing).

So the more I learned about myself as a spiritual being, able to have the best of both worlds, sans "rules," I was pretty excited.

When I got my first clairvoyant reading, I was amazed at how much love and light and empowerment could be squeezed into 60 minutes.

Here I am today having accepted my own gifts and spirituality, no longer hiding from a complete aspect of myself because of dogma or social stigma or fear. And it feels so incredibly FREE!!!!

You know when you can just be your entire full, wonderful self?

How often do you feel you can be truly you?

Standing in your own light and wholeness is nothing but true love, peace, and freedom.

You are a creation of the Universe and were designed perfectly.

All of you is loveable.

And so, to society, I say:

Enough with the stigmas.

Enough with the dogma.

Enough with the judgments.

Enough with dimming your light and truth to fit into societal norms.

Embrace who you truly are. All of you.

Come out of the spiritual closet.

Or any closet you've been hiding pieces of yourself in.

I'm incredibly grateful to be standing in my truth and using my God-given gifts to serve the world. I still pinch myself at the transformations I see in my clients, and I am so grateful I get to do my soul's work full time.

PURPOSE PROMPTS

Where are you holding onto past beliefs or suppressing your natural gifts to fit social constructs or dogmas? Where are you able to shine your light brighter and embrace all of you, all sides of you, and love them all even more?

_____

_____

_____

_____

_____

LOVE IS YOUR NATURAL STATE

Love, believe it or not, is your natural state.

You were born as pure love.

As you grew up, your experiences either confirmed that or you were shown reason to believe otherwise.

These experiences embedded themselves into your identity.

You may believe your truth is the result of your life experiences.

This is not true.

Yes, your experiences shape your personality, your character, your learnings, and your growth, but they are not your deepest truth.

Your deepest truth is love.

Your deepest truth is confidence. Abundance. Compassion. Understanding. Kindness. You are not the stories you carry. You are not your pain. You are not your trauma.

You are not a failure.

I used to believe I wasn't good enough. I thought I was "broken" and "hard work." I lived in a state of constant comparison.

When I had my spiritual awakening, which happened around the time I stopped drinking, I came back to my truth.

I realized I was "allowed" to become the person I am. I realized I was able to embrace full love for myself, others, the planet, all things.

WHAT DOES IT EVEN MEAN TO BE SPIRITUAL?

Release the rules of "what it means to be spiritual."
The most spiritual thing you can do is be yourself.
That doesn't mean be an asshole if you're currently an asshole.

It means tapping into ALL that YOU'RE experiencing, knowing that because you're experiencing it, it's divine, it's perfect, and it's an opportunity to evolve.

When you aim to be love, you learn to love yourself, fully and unconditionally.

As soon as you start comparing yourself or wondering if you're being "spiritual enough" or anything else "enough," you're putting yourself in ego and out of the truth of your heart, which knows no comparison.

When you allow your emotions, feelings, and thoughts to be your greatest teachers of your highest truth, you're honoring your full self, all that you are—shadow and all.

One of my divine clients once shared that she felt she should be "more spiritual" with how she felt about a particular situation.

My heart dropped and opened with so much compassion for her in that moment. The spiritual rules placed upon us by the spiritual community only invite more dogma and stigma and add more boxes to the things from which we're liberating ourselves.

When you aim to be the most loving being you can, you see all things as divine.

When I'm faced with situations I don't know how to handle, or the loving thing to do, I call on my angels to help me.

Sometimes I wonder what Jesus would have done and try to do that.
Sometimes I wonder what Shakti would do and try to do that.

Sometimes I call on Archangel Michael to help with healing or the Angel of Mercy to help me see the best of a situation.

Sometimes I ask Kali.
Sometimes I call my guides.
Oftentimes, I pray to God.

There's no right or wrong way to be spiritual when you surrender to the full truth and take responsibility for your journey.

It's all okay.

You cannot get your personal journey wrong.

We are all human, all doing our best, all seeking love, seeking truth.

There's no need for shaming, labelling, judgment, or anything else—not towards anyone else, and especially not to yourself.

PURPOSE PROMPTS

What does spiritual health look like to you?

_____

_____

_____

_____

How do you now get to begin to enhance your spiritual connection?

_____

_____

REMEMBERING SOVEREIGNTY

I was in Banff, near the beautiful Rocky Mountains in Canada.
I had just facilitated a marriage, a divine union. It was one of the most beautiful weddings I had been to, and the only one I'd officiated (at the time of writing this—watch this space!).
That trip was a time of deep initiation, cosmic remembrance, and spiritual growth.

I was doing my daily energy work, breathwork, and meditation, and all of a sudden, I found myself accessing higher realms. It was like I was going home to remember, so much information flowing through me, bypassing my conscious mind; all I felt was elated, pure, free, love.

It was like a deep knowing that my soul was receiving wisdom from the higher realms and my mind and body would soon catch up. I let go of the mind's need to know exactly what was happening.

A recalibration of truth, accessing the depths of who I am and who I came here to be.

I am light—the embodiment of the divine, an expression of source.

WE ALL ARE.

I choose to get out of my own way and allow myself to be a channel for the highest good of all. I open to love and let all else fade. I see shadow, and I choose love. We all have this choice available to us. It's simply a matter of choice and knowing that we have the choice.

In this particular meditation, I was shown many souls gathered around Earth, which looked like a tiny glowing ball in the middle of us, as we reconnected and remembered our collective mission.

It was like we were pure beings of light, and we were being guided to integrate that which we came onto the planet to be.
A family of souls playing an integral part in raising the collective consciousness. Our bodies receive the message, our DNA shifts frequency as we remember, our souls know what to do.

It is time to activate our missions here on Earth.

Remember: you are at one with the Universe.

You are here to be a channel for divine light.

That means releasing boxes of the mind and society while in this body.

We are not restricted when we are at one with love.

It is a commitment to becoming free of boxes that restrict our beings.

We are not here to be tamed or domesticated.

Even as a wife, partner, or husband, our sovereignty reminds us that we are in union with the Universe, first and foremost, honoring our highest divine will, in divine union honoring this within each other.

It is a choice to release all ego-centric intentions and commit to embodying the fullest expression of our hearts. Simply declare, "Universe, guide me."

Do no intentional harm, and cause no intentional pain. This is often what our biggest obstacles will be. To choose love over convenience. Is love convenient?

No, not always. It knows no bounds.

Is love easy?

From the heart and soul—yes.

From the current constructs of our world, not so much, not yet anyway.

I choose love over convenience. I always trust I will be guided and know what to do. There's no wrong way. There are many timelines, paths, and possibilities all existing at once.

Choose one, choose many, choose love.

When we are living from a place of sovereignty, we remember there is no such thing as obligation. We remember our power to change our minds at any time. To say no to obligation and control and needing permission. We do this and we say yes to our soul.

From here, we say yes to love. From joy, tenderness, and care.
If we make decisions from reluctance or obligation, then what energy are we saying we are okay with in our lives, and on our planet?

I choose to break boxes within my own life of obligation stemming from control.

I feel a huge sense of responsibility with the immense opportunities and time of freedom and liberation we are living in.
A sense of responsibility to live a life of liberation, freedom, and sovereignty, to pave the way and be a voice for those who don't have a voice, and who do not yet have the luxury of freedom as I do. As we do. For the future of humanity. For all who have walked before me, and all those who will walk after me.

So, to those guiding me, I say thank you. To spirit, ancestors, keepers of the Earth, for showing me the way. My next steps, my purpose, and mission on the planet. Thank you for showing me how to tap into my highest state of abundance, love, and joy.

Thank you for showing me how I can be the best channel to bring forth the new earth and for the highest abundance, wealth, and healing of the planet and the people.

Thank you for using me as a channel for change, for light, for love.

My love is eternal.
My heart expansive.
My soul fully expressive.

The world is a reflection of the beauty of your love.

Be open. Be free. You are free. You are love.

We are love.

As I landed back on New Zealand soil, activated with the wisdom of the Rockies and ancient Canadian land, I realized I was back on my homeland with an open heart. The first time I can truly remember, after a lifetime trying to run and hide from myself, I tried to run from my land. I felt a lightness flowing through me, seeing the world through the lens of my heart. I feel the flame of the Universe radiate through my vessel, reminding me that I am love.

I am love, I am love, I am love.

"Creator, help me remember and embody this always, all times, all places, with all people, that I am love."

Our realization of our divine truths happen through a series of our commitments to our own paths.

Each moment we learn, experience, discover, explore, they create a collection of 'knowings' within. When we are ready, in what seems all of a sudden, the "Aha! THIS is who I am" happens.

A PRAYER TO REMEMBER
YOUR HIGHEST CALLING

I call upon the angel of Mercy as I walk this plane,
Bringing compassion, truth, and forgiveness
to embody the essence of divine love for the highest
good of all.
I am the light.
I release my ego and surrender to being a channel for
the divine will that wants to use me for the highest good
of all.
Show me the way
Show me the truth
Show me the light
Great Spirit
And I will follow your guidance, lead, and wisdom.

STOP GIVING AWAY YOUR POWER

Indecision
Waiting for permission
Letting others tell you how to think
Or what to think
Or what to do
We give away our power
Our full knowing
Our deepest wisdom

To all things outside us
Family, friends, doctors, channellers, readers, the media...
Waiting for them to tell us who we are
What to do
And deciding our futures for us

When we look at life and see
That everything is an invitation
To help you reconnect with source

And help you remember
Source is your boss
And you are the creator of your own reality

Now THAT is power.

RECLAIM YOUR POWER

It's so easy to want to be handed the answers.

But true ascension is found when we discover how to find the answers for ourselves.

Growth happens when we overcome obstacles.

If we are constantly seeking guidance external to us, obstacles are much more challenging to navigate when they arise.

Our greatest power, strength, and resilience happens in overcoming challenges.

It requires a huge amount of self-trust to move forward without having external validation.

It requires enormous amounts of faith to take action with nothing but an inner knowledge.

Most of us have been so disconnected from our truth and wait for permission for all decisions we make.

We might have learned this from our childhood, having to ask our caregivers' or parents' permission for all we do... and as adults, we never fully learn how to give ourselves this permission.

It's a massive "rule" to break to go against your own conditioning of seeking outside of yourself for answers and instead, to trust your own ability, your own strength, and your own knowing.

I've found myself in many situations, including with people who have my highest good at heart—like close family or my husband—where I'll want to do something, but ask for their opinion.

And instead of acting upon my own knowing, the part of me still seeking permission and approval listens to their advice.

More often than not, I end up resentful and frustrated that I didn't listen to myself, and instead gave my power away by taking advice that didn't resonate in the first place. But I thought another person might know better than I about a decision I have to make.

To reclaim your power, your sovereignty, and ultimately your freedom requires a level of trusting your inner knowing and having the courage to act upon it.

WE ARE HERE

I opened my arms, my heart wide, feet planted firmly on Mother Earth
as I arched my back and released all I was holding onto.
All I was hiding in my heart.
Opening all that I closed off from the world, from myself.
I released it.
Let it go.

Whooooooooooosh.

I AM HERE.

I AM HERE.

I AM HERE.

To be a channel for divine will, love.

"I AM HERE!" I channeled, the words flowing through me, grounding me here on Earth as I remembered my home in the stars. My divine mission in this life.

The freedom that comes from liberation from human constructs is undeniable.

WE are not here to fit into old boxes, paradigms, rules, belief structures, constructs, or anything else that restricts and limits the truth of who we are.

We are here to RE-CREATE the constructs.

To bring the star wisdom to Mother Earth and anchor in the new grid, new paradigm, new way of being.

We are leading the way.

Breaking patterns & recreating WHOLENESS.

Love, truth, freedom, liberation.

Reclaiming our sovereignty.
The knowing of our divinity.
The realization of our already wholeness.

There are no more rules.

You lead. Your heart leads.

You are here to bring LOVE into the world.

You are the very BEING you believe you are.

You've always felt different, out of place... you're in the right place. You ARE here to do things differently. That "differently" is with love. With light. With grace and gratitude. With forgiveness and compassion.

You are the light.
You are love.

Open up, let it go & let it flow.

You've got this.
I've got you.
I've got you.
You've got you.

LIBERATION

Societal boxes.
Expectations.
Ideals.
Preferences.
The co-dependent needs of others.
Opinions.

In order to fit ourselves into any of these, we create extra layers to fill the gaps that our natural selves do not. We wear masks. We become someone we're not to fit in. Like a mould.
Believing we have to fit in, in order to survive. As children, we learned what upset our parents and our environments, and we learned what pleased them. We did less of what upset others in order to avoid rejection. We did more of what pleased them in order to fit in.

In the process,
all the layers,
masks,
behavior,
habits,

that we picked up,
That are not our own,
We forgot whose they were.
We became convinced
That they were ours.
We wore them
Not knowing how to take them off.
In this process of collection,
We became addicted
To this way of being,
Silently suffering,
Drowning,
While believing
This was life,
This was reality,
This is who we are,
How we be.

Well, my love,
It's time.
To return to sender.
It's time.
To remove the masks.
It's time.
To remember
The truth of all that you are.
The you that needs not explain herself, himself.
The you that knows
Embodies
Your infinite worth,
Your infinite love,
Your infinite magnificence.
When you remove the layers,
It may seem
Your world is crumbling.
The destruction is a recreation,
Unravelling
The layers

That have kept you
From truly knowing
Who you really are.
And as the layers peel back,
All you're left with
Is a you, a world, a life
Without suffering.
This, we call
LIBERATION.

ENERGETIC BOUNDARIES

Our healing journeys, our paths of highest alignment, require us to be free from distractions so we can be free to use our discernment for our highest good, and to listen to our own inner guidance and direction.

My husband and I often do things separately so we can grow together.

He understands I need space, and I understand he needs his.

I need space daily, and I take time each morning to be by myself, in ceremony with my soul and source.

I usually take several hours each week as well, whether it is going to the beach, or the sauna, or simply in my office, meditating, shamanic journeying, dancing.

By communicating our needs, first of all by honoring them to ourselves, it allows those around us to honor this and know not to take it personally.

I notice if I don't create my own space and time to be by myself, I react faster or become more irritable, or feel drained much more easily.

I do myself, and everyone around me a favor and honor my healing journey and my own needs first.

From here, I can give more of myself to those I love and to my clients.

And because I work with energy, I ensure I honor my energy first.
I start my day by clearing my energy field and refilling it with source energy from the Earth's core. I will do mini versions of this several times a day, especially if I've had many client sessions, or I have been doing online trainings or livestreams where lots of people are watching. I'll notice energetic cords come into my field of people who are watching my things online. If I ever forget or don't do my energy work and honor my energetic needs and boundaries and "spiritual hygiene," I can feel really tired or super emotional. Usually, if this is the case, I'll realize what's happened and give myself an "energetic shower."

I first learned the importance of honoring my needs like this and clearing my energy field when I was jam-packing my days, filling them with back to back appointments and then burning out nearly every month. One of my teachers asked how I was clearing my energy from all the work I was doing with people, and also all the people who were sending me thoughts of negativity or jealousy...

I was effectively "wearing" all that energy and taking on board my clients' energy. They left feeling amazing, and I felt so drained!

PURPOSE PROMPTS

How to clear your energy field:

There are several ways you can do this. Choose whichever resonates with you, or create your own:

- Visualize a waterfall of white light from source cleansing your entire body and energy field, and thank mother earth for transmuting this energy and recycling it.

- Use your hands to "wash" your energy field by visualizing healing energy coming from your hands, clearing out any negativity from the past, sending it up to Source to be transmuted, and refilling your energy field with Source energy.

- Imagine a giant magnet above you pulling up all darkness, or anything that doesn't belong in your energy field, and thank Source for absorbing this and replacing it with light.

- After you've cleared your energy field, seal it back up for strength.

- Think of these as spiritual boundaries and hygiene.

Protection:

- Visualize a giant crystal around you, connected all the way to the core of the earth, and all the way up to Source.

- Imagine a large bubble of solid white light around you, encompassing your entire energy body, right into the earth and a meter above your head.

- Use your healing hands to draw a bubble of protective energy around you.

- Your intent is what commands the energy, this may seem simple, yet it works wonders.

Just as you wouldn't let a stranger in your house, you also wouldn't let a stranger send you unwanted energy or use your energy for them. Most of the time, this is unconscious and not malicious, but it happens more often than we know. One of the biggest tell-tale signs that my clients experience when this happens is they feel unusually exhausted, and it's not a physical health issue (I believe all physical health stems from energy before it manifests in the physical body).

After cleansing and implementing protection or "energetic boundaries," and setting new standards to honor their own healing journeys, they notice a massive difference in their energy levels and mood.

How will you now honor your energy, needs, and spiritual hygiene on a daily or weekly basis?

STOP DOUBTING YOUR DREAMS

If you could see the divine orchestration of your dreams becoming reality, all doubt would subside.

In 2017, I'd been granted a week's leave from my job and was on vacation in the Cook Islands. It was my birthday, and Dane and I woke early to do stand-up paddle board yoga on the lagoon at sunrise, walked outside, and saw a shooting star.

I knew magic was unfolding.

I did my usual birthday-journaling... annual reflections and intention setting.

But this time I specifically asked the Universe, "Please show me my purpose. I'm ready."

From then, the days felt long. I felt impatient.
Why was nothing moving?

Fast forward 3½ years later, and I received the gift of hindsight.

Sitting by the pool at my villa in Bali, where I would do my rituals each morning on the beautiful island I was blessed to call "home," I remembered that request I made, only a few years earlier.

I zoomed out and saw the life I created from a higher perspective. A life where I get to mentor, teach, coach, guide, and lead the most divine souls in their soul missions, money, and manifestations, without anyone telling me where to be or what to do... Literally living the life of my dreams.

I can't even remember what it feels like to NOT be living my purpose. Whenever I feel frustrated at why my "NEXT" isn't here yet (lol), I remember this very journey to get to where I am now.

I remember the times I kept going before I could see proof. The times I made decisions, not from where I was, but the person I was BEcoming.

I showed up, even when I was afraid.

As I tell my clients, "Remember and appreciate this time in your life; you'll never get it back." And while you might feel frustrated that your NEXT isn't here, in hindsight, you'll wish you made MORE of these moments of NOW you have been blessed with each day.

So, while I'm excited and grateful for my "next" as I witness it manifest right before my eyes, I simultaneously live in deep gratitude for each day in the NOW, knowing I'll never get these moments back, and they, too, will become moments of things I read in my journal, in my future chapters of this consciously created life.

PURPOSE PROMPTS

How are you choosing to surrender, trust, and have gratitude for your life journey even more?!

_____

_____

_____

_____

Imagine you are now living the life you have been desiring to live. Connect with that future version of you. What wisdom do they want to share with you now?

_____

_____

_____

_____

_____

YOU ARE YOUR GREATEST TEACHER

you seek external to yourself
looking for someone to save you
to take away your pain
to tell you what to do

but what you don't realize
is that you are the only one with all the pieces

no one teacher will help you find
all that you are looking for

for you are your greatest teacher.

When you give yourself permission to trust yourself, your intuition, your gut instinct, your inner guidance, you reclaim the piece of you that you've been searching for your whole life. We are here experiencing this life and exploring our depth through the duality, the contrast, the polarity. Every experience brings a lesson.
Every obstacle evokes an opportunity for growth. We are here to experience the fullness of being human. The dark and the light, and from there, getting to decide how we want our lives to feel.

But here's the thing.

No one can take away our suffering.
Not a lover
Not a friend
Not a coach
Not a therapist
Not a TV show
Not a Facebook post
Not a "like"
Not anyone else but you.

I used to try anything I could get my hands on to numb my pain. In the long run, it made it worse. The only way we fully heal is through navigating our way home to ourselves, within ourselves.

In my moments of dark nights of the soul, the loneliness was so loud.

It didn't matter how many people I had around me, teachers, coaches, friends, loved ones, even strangers inside Facebook groups... I still felt so alone.

What we don't realize in those moments is where our greatest strength comes from.

Those of us who are tasked with big missions in helping this world be a more love-filled place will experience deep pain.
This is where our deepest strength and resilience is born, as we learn to experience pain without suffering, and let it guide us to our highest truth.

Reclaiming freedom and sovereignty is an inner job. One that no one can do for us.

In these moments where we feel so disconnected from Source, and can't even feel the love of the Universe, it feels like we are well and truly just left to suffer, that no one cares, and what's the point of it all anyway?

When I started on my healing journey, I would seek for people to feel sorry for me.

When I didn't receive the sympathy I was seeking or my pain was still there, I would get mad at them... Trying to find an outlet or something or someone to blame for my pain.

Our growth and healing for us to step into our greatness doesn't happen in the moments of celebration.

It happens in the deep conflict between our own ego and soul.

The moments of the breakdown before the breakthrough.

The feeling helpless laying on the floor before the hint of light starts to shine through.

The only way to fully heal...
To fully love...
Is to feel...
To experience the humanness of every experience.

And let the distant whisper of our soul remind us...

This is ALL happening FOR us.

Together we heal (even when it feels like we are alone), together we rise (even when it feels like we are alone), together we co-create the new earth (where we are far from alone).

When you remember this, you remember you ARE your greatest teacher.

PART SIX: YOU'RE MORE POWERFUL THAN YOU'LL EVER KNOW

MANTRA FOR SUCCESS

Thank You Universe,
For this incredible life I live.
For the abundance I am,
the people I serve,
and the impact I make,
As I step deeper into my purpose.

Thank you for always guiding me
and bringing Magic
into each and every day.

I surrender to your highest guidance to flow through me
for my greatest life experience.

Abundance, love, health, joy, wealth, freedom, peace,
incredible experiences, opportunity.

Thank you for showing me the way.

Thank you for the experiences you've brought to me
so far,
Helping me to grow and know my own strength.
Thank you for all that I've already magnetized,
And all that is being magnetized to me.

Thank you for amazing relationships,
Amazing people in my life,
And the abundance of things I desire
Flowing my way.

Thank you for all of it.
I know it is all happening in divine timing.
Thank you.
I'm so grateful to be impacting humanity in my highest

way possible.
To facilitate and co-create positive change
For generations to come,
And to be blessed with such divine abundance.

Liberated from any constraints to enjoy the full bliss of this human experience.

Thank you, thank you, thank you.

SELF WEALTH

Self-wealth: total alignment of mind, body, and soul, knowing that money manifests from here.

Creating a life of self-wealth requires your soul's empire to be built on solid foundations. It is all very well to manifest money and amazing things, but if you are building on shaky grounds, the tower will tumble.

You are here on this journey of a magnificent life for, well, life. You've got this and there is no rush.

You're setting yourself up for the long run. There is no get rich quick scheme. If you are chasing the end goal, you'll miss your life along the way. Our greatest wealth comes from the alignment of your mind + body + soul, stepping fully into your purpose and making a magnificent impact ONCE YOU ARE IN ALIGNMENT WITH YOUR WHOLE SELF.

This means releasing ALL that no longer serves you. Everything.

Sometimes this will mean your life will turn upside down.

Sometimes this will mean relationships will end.

Sometimes this will mean you will uncover and have to process a whole bunch of suppressed emotions and traumas you've been carrying around that are blocking the truth of who you are and preventing you from being the fullest expression of yourself.

Ever feel awkward in social situations?

Or replay conversations over and over in your mind, days after you've had them, wishing you could have shown up differently?

Or perhaps you feel a twinge of jealousy when you see #squadgoals on Instagram, wishing you had something similar. Perhaps you feel no one even knows the "real you," not even you?

These come about because we have un-consciously locked away whole aspects of who we are.

When we truly know ourselves, and truly love ourselves, these things slowly disappear. We unlock a part of ourselves hidden often for a lifetime. And when we see the full capacity of WHO we are, in the entirety of our true magnificence, never again will we shut ourselves off from others, from the world, from our greatest life... which is waiting on the other side of hiding.

From there, once we've stopped hiding from the world and from ourselves, miracles happen.

CREATIVES, THIS IS YOUR CALLING

How many times do you hear people say, "I don't have much money because I'm a creative, struggling artist, or [insert reason here]"?

This is a paralyzing belief, confirmed by the mind over and over and over again by circumstance and current realities, cemented in this cycle by experiences and perceptions, which create more cause for this belief, and the cycle continues, often through communities, societies, and passed down through generations.

It's time to break this cycle.

With the way the world is, the creative solutions to complex problems are going to heal this planet.

Creatives have the keys to success with the new earth we are creating. I know artists who don't just paint "pretty pictures," they channel messages that are visual activations on a soul-deep level that allow the viewer to access new parts of themselves so THEY (the viewer) can show up in their life with higher alignment of THEIR soul path and do what THEY came to this world to do.

Photographers who don't just "shoot nice images"—they capture the essence of someone's TRUE beauty so that person can, in turn, see their inner beauty reflected back at them and remember their true magnificence, so THEY can show up with more confidence in their life and do things that REQUIRE confidence (following your purpose when society tells you to do otherwise).

Fashion designers who are creating solutions to the global damage the fast fashion industry has contributed to.

Dancers who incorporate dance and movement therapy as a way to help people heal and access deeper parts of their own intuition.

Graphic designers who support conscious entrepreneurs in THEIR missions.

Writers who write concepts and messages SO profound, they could change the lives of millions if they could just get their message out in the world.

Entrepreneurs who see the world wearing a full time "problem solving hat," and are constantly seeking ways to improve things / help people / the planet / animals.

Healers who are craving peace on earth and know that it starts with us as individuals to find our own inner peace and freedom, and through that comes the ability to guide others to do the same.

(And sooo much more).

Money is a creative energy that amplifies whatever we want it to amplify, and acts as a resource to leverage your impact and soul mission.

Creatives, come out of hiding.
Life is your canvas, and the world is waiting for your exhibition.

Truly leading from our hearts requires being liberated from the limitations of our minds, so we can rise together in bringing through all that's required for this new earth, for generations to come.

PURPOSE PROMPTS

Observe how much time you give to "creation" or how deeply you actually honor the ways your soul desires to be expressed.

Schedule a creative date with yourself. Whether it is painting, writing, singing, pottery, dancing, photography, music. Whether you try something new or pick a hobby or creative project you loved as a kid.

Notice your energy and when you feel most alive. This is an indicator of your own personal alignment and can also give clues to your purpose.

I feel most alive when:

_____

_____

_____

_____

When I was a kid, I loved to:

_____

_____

_____

_____

I notice myself enjoying life the most when:

_____

_____

_____

_____

ABUNDANCE ACTIVATION

The greatest key to abundance is to own your full power. Own who you are, focus on yourself. Don't worry about others' judgments, or what they might think.

My Mom used to have a quote on her fridge that has stuck with me ever since:

"Comparison kills contentment"
- anonymous

You are a powerful creator. When coming from a place of love, there is no greed.

Everything is energy, and you can create your dream reality, your next level of success, abundance, and wealth by choosing to embody the thoughts and feelings of that energy.

Thoughts become things.

Everything that has ever been created started with a thought.

Choose your thoughts. Create your dreams. Own your full power.

Place a hand on your heart, take a deep breath into the bottom of your stomach, fill your heart with the oxygen you breathe and read the below aloud, or in your mind's voice:

I am grounded.
I am free.
I am love.
I am guided.
I am powerful.
I am abundant.
I am a miracle.
I am alive.
I am a child of the Universe.
I am grateful for life.
I am grateful for today.
I am appreciating all that I already have, and all that I already am.
I am abundant.

And so it is.

FINDING FREEDOM

"Someone saying they are not spiritual is like a cube of ice saying it is not water."

- said by a teacher of mine

My soul seeks a freedom I can't explain.

The type of freedom that can only be experienced when you are living your truth.

The type of freedom that can only be experienced when you are being your most authentic self.

The type of freedom that can only be experienced when you listen to your own intuition instead of the opinions of others.

The type of freedom that can only be experienced when you say what you mean and not what you think you should say.

The type of freedom that can only be experienced when you chase your own dreams and goals, and not others' expectations.

The type of freedom that can only be experienced when you stand tall, stand proud, and say, "This is me. This is who I am," and don't wait for a response of acceptance from others.

This is my journey.

A journey of freedom.

Of love. Of passion. Of peace. Of acceptance. Of gratitude. Of expansion. Of joy. And, of course, fun.

The sense of freedom that can be found in knowing and understanding your journey is unexplainable.

Purposeful.

If you are ready to join me in your own journey of freedom, expansion, divine self-love, and complete inner peace, hear the call of your soul. Your freedom is waiting.

To create your dream life, you've gotta be meticulous with what you focus on.

What do you spend most of your time thinking about, speaking about, worrying about, or getting excited about?

This is a clear indicator of where your biggest focus currently is.

If you're wanting to live differently than you currently are, it requires you to think, behave, and act differently.

If you spend your time picking things apart, complaining, trying to figure out WHY things are the way they are, you put your energy into that instead of doing something about it.

All things are thoughts before they are things.

Everything in this world is manifested from what was first a thought or the vibration of a thought.

When you realize you're feeding your worries, doubts, fears, or limitations by focusing on them more often than the direction you're WANTING to go, simply make peace with the past and realize the MAGNIFICENCE that you are, and your innate ability to change at any given moment.

PURPOSE PROMPTS

Find Your Freedom

What does freedom mean to you?

_____

_____

_____

_____

When we talk about freedom, it is important to also consider fulfilment. Freedom comes from a place of inner contentment, which goes hand in hand with fulfilment, which goes hand in hand with happiness.

What does fulfilment mean to you?

_____

_____

_____

_____

When do you feel the most fulfilled?

_____

_____

_____

_____

What are 5 ways you can bring more fulfilment and freedom into your life?

_____

_____

_____

_____

_____

What do you believe is stopping you from living this right now?

_____

_____

_____

_____

_____

Now that you can see what you believe is stopping you, what will you choose to do?

_____

_____

_____

_____

7 STEPS TO CREATING YOUR DREAM LIFE

1. ENVISION

Teach your mind what to focus on. Focus on where you are going. Use visualization techniques, create a vision board, write daily affirmations, give yourself permission to dream bigger.

2. ACCOUNTABILITY

Know the power of having a support system that will help hold you accountable. Whether it be a mentor, coach, support group, a declaration, visibility of goals, having your vision board right next to your bed, post-it notes around the house, or any of the techniques you've learned in this book.

3. PATIENCE

Change is a daily practice. It can take 30, 60, 90 days to solidify a habit—and sometimes longer depending on the DEPTH of change. Whatever change you are creating, focus on ONE DAY AT A TIME.

4. CELEBRATION

CELEBRATE each mini milestone you hit. It doesn't matter how you celebrate, it's the energy and excitement of celebration that teaches your system to continue with your new way of being, as you reward your new habits. New neurological pathways are formed and strengthened, and your new habits will soon become subconscious— in time, they will begin to feel "effortless" as you re-create your new "normal."

5. HOLD FAITH AND PERSEVERANCE

When you're doing all this work, making big (or little) changes, your brain wants instant reward. The truth is, fulfilling change can feel like you're doing a lot of work for minimal return. Not a great ROI in the early stages. But with perseverance, the time, energy, and efforts that you invest now will give you a HUGE return later.

This FAITH is knowing that everything you're doing now IS going to pay off in the future. You don't even necessarily need to KNOW what that looks like, but you know it's better than where you've been.

6. A STRONG WHY

When the going gets tough, you've gotta remember WHY you're doing this. Remember back to the reasons you wrote at the beginning of this book.

7. RELEASE CONTROL AND LET THE UNIVERSE LEAD

When you start out, your goals might be one thing. As you go on your journey, you'll be directed and redirected, over and over again. That's the beauty of life. If you set an intention, do all that you're guided to in order to make it happen, and when it has run its course, allow yourself to shift course. Going with the flow and being unattached to outcomes, while having a strong intention, will set you up for lasting, inner happiness.

As you come into higher alignment and higher vibration, what you're capable of also "increases--" this means the goals you were working towards no longer feel in your HIGHEST alignment... It is up to you whether you shift, but if you continue to hold onto something just because "you were told in a reading," or "you had a vision," you may LIMIT what you're actually here to create, experience, and BE.

BE OKAY WITH CHANGE

What do you TRULY want to do? What's stopping you?

We'll often look to all external things that may be "obstacles," but in reality, the only person stopping us, is us.

Remember that all obstacles are growth-provoking opportunities, and we get to reinvent ourselves to rise above the obstacles and see them as tools to help us in our transformations and growth, rather than preventing us.

Each new chapter we enter requires a new version of ourselves. This doesn't mean we lose ourselves, but rather, we become fuller expressions of our most authentic selves, and release the stuff that wasn't ours, that's not serving us, in the first place.

If you don't want to change, ask yourself... why?.

Fear of judgment? Fear of rejection? Fear of failure?

One of the biggest blockers to our best life is our fears getting in the way.

One of the most important parts of an unlimited life—a truly wealthy life—is choosing FAITH over FEAR every single time.

If you are making decisions in fear, you are choosing limitations. You are choosing to let your fight / flight / freeze response choose your life for you.

Ask yourself this, "If you had everything your way, what would your life look like?!"

Visualize what you desire, get clear on what you want, focus on that.

PRACTICE GRATITUDE.

PRACTICE FORGIVENESS.

PRACTICE FLUIDITY.

PRACTICE NON ATTACHMENT.

Approach your life and all the shifts happening with an attitude of "it is what it is." Your vibration is your greatest asset, and by simply observing all things that are happening rather than letting external situations take power over you, you're able to hold your light, maintain your power and sovereignty, and unlock your manifestation power in your emotional mastery.

INTERNAL vs EXTERNAL VALIDATION

You're changing for you, first and foremost. While someone or something might be a motivator for you, ultimately, it is for you to be the best you, so you can bring more love into the world in the way you best know how.

Begin practicing receiving internal validation rather than relying on external situations for your sense of worth or value.

When you do this, you'll reclaim power over the external world and begin to learn the secrets of creating your reality from within.

You are in charge of your inner state. You get to cultivate your power from within and receive the love you desire from within, too.

Remember, you are here on Earth—you're a divine creation of the Universe. You belong here, and you are so loved. When you truly feel this, and learn how to feel this, you will discover your limitless nature and infinite potential.

Your greatest sense of worth, value, and self comes from within.

LEARN FLUIDITY AND NON ATTACHMENT

When I was in the early days of my addiction recovery journey, I spent a lot of time in nature. While I was learning how to be human and to be alone in my own mind with no escape, I would walk the bush tracks behind my house at the time, hearing the sounds of water trickling down the stream, smelling the moist ground of the forest after rain fall, and observing the rhythm of mother Earth. I spent time with the trees and watching birds, learning more from them in the space of a few months than I learned anywhere else in years.

And for that reason, rather than writing this piece of the chapter, I invite you to go outside and spend time with nature, in the ways you desire, and receive the wisdom only Mother Earth can bring you—the sort of wisdom you can't read about in a book. Spend time with the ocean or trees or rocks or flowers and watch the natural environment around you. Learn, observe, be, and practice embodying what you learn.

TAP INTO YOUR CREATIVITY

Do you consider yourself creative?

We're all creative, whether we believe it or not. Part of unlocking your purpose is about tapping into your creativity. It is about bringing through new solutions to old problems.

Creating solutions, creating new ways of being, creating a new path in your life or business.

It doesn't matter how you express your purpose; following joy is what's most important.

Often trying to figure it out is what's preventing us—labels and words. Your purpose is an essence, an energy. It's always of service... primarily to People, Planet, or Animals. And it's a form of art. A creative flow of energy. I believe even science is an art form; our brains computing information received from our creative, infinite, channel—the part of us that "sees" answers to problems or overcomes obstacles without knowing exactly "how'".

Our souls have a desire to express themselves, and our lives are the canvas.

If you're a creative, you might carry the story of the "poor artist."

The truth is, people aren't buying your product or service; they're buying what it brings them. They're purchasing your craft based on the value they perceive it to hold.

Your story, your message, your transformation, you BEING the example of positive change and light in the world... that is the essence of our output. YOU are the walking testimony of your own medicine.

You are proof it is possible to change, to see results.

There is a time and place for qualifications, but through your innate ability to create, you are bringing through things in anew way.

The way of the future isn't the way of the past.

We are RE-CREATING the future of our planet, our way of being, our world.

There are people reading this who will likely be CREATING things to be taught in universities and professional capacities...it requires you following your heart and the truth of your soul.

Your life is your story, your medicine, your power...YOU are the gateway to bringing love into the world.

Choose FAITH over FEAR.

And one step at a time.

One day at a time.

CELEBRATE SUCCESS

Celebrate all of your successes. Allow yourself to feel proud of yourself. It's a complete expression and acknowledgement of self-love. Celebrate your wins, no matter how big or small they seem. If they feel like an achievement, then they ARE!! Never compare your journey to anyone else's.

Never compare your accomplishments to anyone else's.

What's big for you may not be big for someone else, and vice versa. And that's totally okay!

You are you, and you're the only person who's lived your life. You get to decide how important something is to you; no one else gets to tell you otherwise.

You decide.

Your wins.

Your journey.

Your success.

Your goals.

Your habits.

Your happiness.

Your ups and downs.

You.

Drop the comparison and pick up the self-compassion.

Big successes are the accumulation of small wins and habit changes, so celebrate them all!! Look how far you've come! And look how far you'll go!

You.

A beautiful way to keep motivated for big goals is to acknowledge all the small wins. Your wins.

Keep going, you.

You've got this.

You do.

OPEN THE GATEWAY TO SUCCESS

How do you know if it's time to rise?

You just know.

You can't ignore the pulsating desire running through your cells.

It's encoded in your DNA, and as you receive the light codes penetrating your aura every single day, the call gets louder.

And stronger.

And more frequent.

"Yeah but what? And HOW?"

Most people get stuck here and stop.

But not you, not I, not us.

The sacred keepers of the new earth.

Galactic wisdom holders and planetary activators.

Paving the way for generations to come.

Helping humanity in every way you can and delving into your darkness to emerge from the flames that have burned your collective entanglement of the matrix forever.

Altering time.

Playing with reality as you once knew it.

And opening the gateway to your deepest success.

The portal of desire flirting with you with her quantum field of infinite possibilities.

Your soul remembers.

Your soul knows.

The HOW of your mind, doesn't matter to your soul.

The HOW is to not know HOW and leap anyway.

To be so fucking invested in your mission and let the burning desire guide you.

Your success is determined by your courage to say yes.

Yes to the whisper.

Yes to the call.

And so, the question isn't, "Are You Ready?"

(You've been ready your whole life).

But rather: ARE YOU LISTENING?

PART SEVEN: CREATING THE NEW EARTH

THE COLLECTIVE CHRYSALIS

Our planet is changing.

Our lives are changing.

Humanity is changing.

We are going through a collective transformation.

We are in a collective chrysalis.

Huge changes in habits, behaviors, patterns, chapters closing, relationships ending, truths being revealed, confusion arising as dust settles. The changes are real and they're happening for your highest good. The times of the past are no longer how we are living our future.

There is no place for lies, manipulation, or control.

This time has been predicted by the ancients.

It's exciting.

What a time to be alive.

Together, as we heal our collective wounds, sexual traumas, inner children, ancestral patterns, past lives, we create vibrational space for love to flood in.

Now is the time to use your deepest discernment.

Listen to your inner guidance, always leading you to your truth.

Conflict is the contrast required to highlight your truth.

Allow things to be as they are and release attachment, mindful not to disrupt the flow of old things as they unravel to create opportunity for what's to come. Beautiful times ahead, deeper anchoring of truth, allow yourself to be with yourself throughout this process.

Trust what you know in your heart to be true, practice compassion and forgiveness while strengthening your own boundaries.

I, too, have been shedding layers, people, habits, thought patterns, and beliefs that are no longer in alignment with where I'm heading. Allowing a grieving of what once was, forgiveness of self for trusting based on soul truths, rather than human truths.

As I step into new levels of awareness, I can no longer ignore the truths being revealed around me, and as I continue to have courage to stand up for myself and what I believe in, people don't always like it, and that's okay.

Conflict arises for change to occur.

I'm no longer letting my past self cling to false truths; rather, I'm letting the divine within lead.

If you, too, are feeling this call to practice deeper discernment and have courage to take action based on the whispers of your heart, then you, too, will be ready and aligned for all the magic and beauty that flows when you do.

The new earth we are transforming into brings us a new energy as a collective, a new portal where energy is the ruling form of communication, and you can't make up energy.

Practice now, listen deeper, and find refuge in the whispers of your soul.

We are at the time of collective awakening.

We are finding our way to truth and love.

This can be one of the most painful things we experience.

All that you have been experiencing is the removal of old, or the exposure of truths, forcing you into deeper growth and ascension.

Surrender and releasing control is an important part of this process, as individuals and as a collective.

When I look at this energetically, it looks like there's a giant magnet in the cosmos pulling up all the darkness from our planet.

Like a collective arrow being removed, as if it is being pulled out, it can feel paaaaainful.

Things to remember are:

- You are learning to have full personal responsibility for life. If you feel like the rug has been pulled from beneath your feet, you're learning to find new balance. This is part of your liberation and freedom. It is found only through personal responsibility. You will only find out the true meaning of this phrase when you are ready. Or, shall we say: when you choose to be ready.

- As unpleasant as much of this seems, it is essential for growth.

- The only way to fully heal is to feel.

- No longer can you ignore or suppress your emotions by keeping busy or ignoring the constant ping of underlying discomfort, anxiety, or uneasiness.

- Many of us are carrying childhood and ancestral energy and emotions that were never expressed, instead suppressed.

- This is why you may feel this deep un-easiness in much of your day-to-day life. Perhaps you got so used to it, you don't even notice it as abnormal anymore.

- You've been presented with situations (opportunities) lately that feel like they've dug up the deepest pain and emotions from within and left you naked in the vulnerability of raw emotion.

- You might've even been searching for people or situations to blame, even if that person is yourself.

- Firstly, this is not a time for blame; rather, it is the time for the removal of shame, guilt, blame, victimhood. Instead, it is a time to find your own inner unity, peace, and wholeness.

Some helpful ways to navigate this:

Feel it. Yes, it's painful. Be present with it. We're conditioned to believe emotions are "bad," so we downplay or ignore them. This only suppresses them more.

Cry, feel, process.

Write letters without the intention of delivering them if you need to get things off your chest but are not able to have a conversation. Burn or throw away after.

Journal.

Feel the emotions; they've been suppressed so long they're coming up to come out.

Move your physical body.

Meditate. Pray.

Get out in nature.

Listen to music or search podcasts on the topic you're experiencing/navigating.

Hearing others in similar situations can help remove loneliness. Inner child healing, shamanic journeying, breathwork, ecstatic dance, boxing, energy work, yoga, qi gong.

Take things one day at a time. Even, one hour, or one minute at a time.

It's one thing to feel emotion and another to project this onto others. Learn the difference, and learn how to forgive... both yourself and others.

These are tools I used to overcome addiction and depression, and continue to use in my own journey and to help others in theirs.
Even if you've been on a healing journey a long time, right now, you are presented with opportunities to go deeper and release all that's still anchoring you in the density of the old way of being, provoking a suffering or internal drama you'd become silently addicted to.

Your instinct will be to suppress it, to avoid pain. You might even put on Netflix or eat or do anything you can to distract yourself from it. This only amplifies it and creates feelings of anxiety, depression, or other dis-ease.

Most importantly, if you can get to a place of forgiveness and compassion, good. It's okay if this part takes a while.

The biggest thing to remember is that YES, while it can seem unfair or like you wish someone would just take away your pain, you are the only one who can heal you.

We all have choices... to blame, ignore, or wish things weren't happening. Or, to take responsibility for ourselves and do whatever it takes to take control of our minds, thoughts, and wellbeing. I love Eckhart Tolle's words, "you are not your thoughts, you are the awareness of your thoughts."

The only way to heal is to feel.

Love yourself through this process. Remove all shame-guilt-resentment. This becomes the ego's way to keep you held back. Let these emotions teach you, but once you see what they've taught you, make peace with the past.

You're not here to suffer in suffering.

This is a time of liberation to your highest truth. The only way there is through truth. You cannot by-pass your way to the truth. It is looking at the darkness, knowing you're the light.

Be brave, have courage, breathe.

When we know ourselves more through our own healing, we access deep joy, deep fulfilment, deep love, and deep states of bliss and abundance.

PURPOSE PROMPTS

YOU NOW GET TO CHOOSE. What is the new earth you want to see? How can you begin letting go of what you know with your mind to begin creating your life from your heart and soul? How do you want humans to treat each other, animals, and the planet? What can you take responsibility for changing within yourself first, and how will you begin to embody these changes? Remember, we are human. One thing and one day at a time. And hold yourself in compassion through this process! This is life, this is why we are here! There's nothing more important than living!

_____

_____

_____

_____

_____

_____

A WAR ON LOVE

Whether you know it or not, there is a battle taking place.
A war, of sorts.
Dark versus light.
Control versus freedom.
Evil versus good.

You may feel it. It's happening right in front of us, and it's been happening for a long time. Many benevolent forces (angels,beings of light) are working with us here in the collective and in the astral realms. In dream state, many of us are working with these forces as part of our soul missions; perhaps you, too?

You might be noticing strangely realistic things happening in your dreams that you can't piece together. Each night, many of us in our astral bodies are confronting the darkness with our light.

You might notice the physicalization of the darkness which starts with control, through fear and manipulation. It is important to use your own discernment. To learn to think for yourself. To begin asking questions and reading between what's NOT being covered, especially in mainstream media. I always encourage my clients and community to think for themselves, ask their own questions, and do their own research. You're encouraged to gather your own information and formulate your own beliefs.

We're in one of the most pivotal moments in human history as we know it. A time that's been predicted for thousands of years (and we get to be here for it!).

It is up to us to decide our destiny.
It is no longer a luxury to use our voices, but a necessity.
A necessity to shine our light.
To hold love and to be the brightest, strongest lights we can be.

Remember, there is no need to fear. Your soul has been preparing a long time for this.

Feel the call
Wake up
Rise
Heal
Choose
Love
Freedom
Truth
Sovereignty

Ask questions. Feel what you on a soul level know to be true.
Question things that seem "off."
And hold your light. Have faith. We are rising. We are awakening.

We are creating heaven on earth.

Now is the time to awaken from our collective slumber.

Rise.

PURPOSE PROMPTS

Many of my clients receive messages and insights in dreams. Before I even started my healing journey, for most of my life, I would receive messages in dreams. Some from loved ones (mostly my grandfather, who was one of my spirit guides for many years), some from other spiritual guides. My spiritual journey began mostly because of the intensity of my dreams and unexplainable situations. I recommend keeping a "dream journal" specifically to record dreams, or messages you receive in dream state.

Your guides are always communicating with you, and often, dream time is easiest for them to give guidance, as we are free from the busy-ness and inner noise of our waking day. If you don't usually remember your dreams, simply request in your mind or in prayer before sleep to remember dreams upon waking. As soon as you wake up, try to record your dream before your brain fully comes to waking consciousness. At first, many things you receive or dreams that you record may not make sense or have any relevance. That's okay. Trust that over time they will (some messages I have received in dream state have no relevance until months—or in some cases, years—later).

IT'S TIME, TO CREATE A NEW EARTH

It's time. You've been preparing for this for longer than you know. The evolution of humanity here on planet Earth. The power of the planet and the cosmos merges through the essence of your love.

Remember this: "I am here, I am the Universe".
See not with your eyes, but through the truth of your heart.
Thank you for the gift of all that you are and bring.
Together, we will move mountains.
We already are.
Recreating an already existing reality, embodying the new earth.
The cosmic energy reminding us of our existence.
Pure, whole, and free.
Love with all of your being.
Embody your mission to remind others of the way.
Thank you, thank you, thank you.
Above the clouds, we are soaring through vortexes of reality. Choosing timelines with our yes's and no's.
Practicality and logic not wanting to be remembered in the expansive bliss of our complete wholeness. Your divinity shines in all that you do.
Remember, everything is sacred.
Awaken, your cosmic remembrance.
Can you see what you're here to do?
The symbols in the stars, the cosmology of truth guiding you.
Earth's medicine showing you, guiding you, healing you.
See the signs and clues as you thank your ancestors, the land,

the earth.
Feel your expansiveness, remember who you are, and why
you're here.
Why we are here.
What are you hiding in your heart, dear soul?
Open. Breathe. Let it go.
Let all the beings who guide you know:

"*I AM HERE!*"

Feel the freedom that comes from the liberation of current
human constructs.

It's undeniable.

We are not here to fit into old boxes, paradigms, belief structures,
constructs, or any other thing that limits the truth of who we are.
We are here to recreate the constructs. To bring the star wisdom
to Mother Earth and anchor in the new paradigm, the new way of
being. We are leading the way. Breaking patterns and
recreating wholeness.

We are reclaiming our sovereignty. The knowing of our divinity.
The realization of our already wholeness.
There are no more rules.
We aren't destroying the old ways. That word is too harsh.
We bring through light, love, and pay attention to the energy our
specific words carry.
Meticulous and intentional in our approach to what we speak.
Awareness of our greater impact.
Awareness of the power that comes from our awareness, when
living from a place of love.

Pay attention to those right in front of you.
Listen with your entire body.
Be aware of your own body, your energy.

When you are tapped into your true self, you have a magnificent gift to impact many, in profound ways. By listening, being kind, they will remember you and forever say, "thank you."

When we truly operate from a place of ultimate intention, we will change the world.
This is the importance of ceremony, mindfulness.
Life becomes one big meditation and commune with the Universe.
Every encounter and interaction is sacred.
Treat it as such.

Your energy and presence are magnetizing, and being around you, people are filled with deep appreciation and a capacity to unlock their own magnificence.
This type of gift cannot be explained with logic.

It just is.

Free from judgment, jealousy, and fear. Just pure compassion and kindness.
May you remember your gift of unconditional love.

And so it is.

THE COSMIC REMEMBRANCE

Let this activate you into remembering who you are, who you came here to be, and set an intention to call in your soul brothers and sisters here to support you in your journey

No longer do you have to do this alone

You are far from alone

We all are together

This is the Cosmic Remembrance

In a world fuelled by the questions of navigation
our worlds connect, surpassing time and space
a cosmic collision of pure consciousness
pure love as our galactic selves give us this gift of remembrance
a feeling of safety as our souls unite
the liberation and freedom we were so afraid of losing
now anchored in our very DNA
we thought we walked this Earth alone
now together as we navigate the illusion of separation
and become the human embodiment of
ONENESS.

let your heart thrust open, after a life shut tight here, you will know
you are home
you've found your way home.

Thank you for reminding me who I am,
and how to access my superpower of love
These activations will awaken all those you encounter,
and you just being you is your greatest superpower
our souls dance as we access lifetimes,
travelling through the cosmos
remembering all the pieces
remember: your love unlocks wonders
and as the world receives this gift,
you'll see where it leads
the divine plan is so profound!

This is the Cosmic Remembrance
as we co-create the new earth.

The end.

ACKNOWLEDGEMENTS

Regan Hillyer, my beautiful mentor. Thank you SO MUCH for everything you have done for Dane and I, for believing in me and opening so many opportunities for me, for living your highest purpose and showing me what's truly possible.

Brian, my first ever mentor. You helped change the trajectory of my entire life, supported me through some of my darkest moments, and helped shape me into the leader I am today. I give thanks to you, more than you will ever know.

Lauren Till, and the whole team at Have It All Publishing. Thank you so much for your guidance, patience, support, and the countless messages and emails back and forth that have gone on behind-the-scenes to get this book into the hands of each person who reads it.

Jason and the team, thank you for the incredible role you play in helping my life's purpose and mission run smoothly! Here's to many more years of success, laughter, and creating a positive impact in the world!

To my clients and students. Thank you for showing up for yourselves, your missions, your families, and the world, and for the courage, love and depth you choose to walk with every single day. I feel so blessed and privileged to be a part of your healing and success journeys.

To my extended family, friends, and community. Thank you to every single one of you. I treasure each of you so much and appreciate you deeply. I'm so grateful to have you in my life, and for the love and uniqueness each of you bring, I could write a whole book just filled with gratitude and the special connections I have with each of you. Thank you for being you.

Anneke, thank you for being the most supportive friend a girl could ask for and for your courageous honesty when I needed it most. I'm so looking forward to many more of life's adventures with you and I'm sure we'll manifest living in the same town together again someday!

Dad, thank you for believing in me and my potential from such a young age. Thank you for teaching me how to choose my attitude, for introducing me to personal development as a little girl, and for teaching me how to set and achieve any goal I put my mind to.

Brittany and Victoria, thank you for being the best sisters I could ever wish for—for your wisdom, support, humour, love, and for being my rocks, more than you know.

Nana, I'm so grateful for you and all of the chats we get to have. Thank you for the gift of being your granddaughter. Pyjama, pyjama.

Mum, thank you for staying with me there at the hospital on *that night* and in those excruciating days that followed, and beyond. For loving me unconditionally and always being there for me. Thank you for teaching me kindness, resilience, self-belief, and integrity, and for showing me how to choose truth, even when it requires massive faith and courage. I love you to the moon and back.

My incredible husband, Dane, where do I even find the words? Thank you for witnessing me at my worst, being there in my darkest hours, and loving me through it all. I feel like the luckiest woman alive to have you by my side and thank the Universe every day for the life we are now creating together. Thank you for always holding down the fort while I write and create, and for saying yes to so many of my crazy ideas. How amazing is life?! I love you so much!

To you, the reader. Thank YOU for being here, for doing the work, and for being on this journey. It takes a special kind of person to do this deep work, and I hope these pages serve you well, and that hearing insights into my journey helped you feel less alone, and more empowered in yours. I trust that from here, the insights you've had into your own truth, and the tools you've received for your healing, will help you in creating a life of deep, lasting happiness and a huge sense of fulfilment in living your life's purpose.

Together we heal, together we rise, together we create Heaven on Earth.

ABOUT THE AUTHOR

Libby Robertson is an author, teacher, entrepreneur, Shamanic healer and life and business coach for conscious leaders who are passionate about making a positive difference in this world.

After realising the Western approach to addiction recovery couldn't provide Libby with the answers she was seeking, she turned to alternative practices which not only helped her to heal, but completely transformed every area of her life and the way that she saw the world. Now passionate about normalising spirituality in the Western world, Libby brings a fresh and grounded approach to business, leadership, success, and living our life's purpose.

Libby is a science graduate, with a major in Psychology. She has professional leadership and management experience, certifications in adult facilitation and education and has completed an apprenticeship as a Shamanic Healer. Libby has healed herself from trauma, addiction and bulimia, completely turning her entire life around. From this background experience, Libby has created a successful global company and brings a unique wealth of wisdom and expertise to her coaching and teaching.

Libby is the CEO of Libby Robertson Global and has co-founded the School of Spiritual Healing Arts (SOSHA) with her husband Dane. Within SOSHA they support their clients and students based all over the world, to create success in their lives, leadership, business and spiritual journeys - in a totally holistic manner.

Together, Libby and Dane have created several social initiatives and charity projects in the last few years, including Hope2Fam, Leaders Making A Difference and The Self Wealth Project. These initiatives aim to give back to the community and promote more love in the world.

After nearly a decade of travelling and moving globally, Libby now lives beside her beloved ocean, in her home country of New Zealand.

MORE BY LIBBY

If you have loved this journey inside 'How To UnMess Your Life' and you want to explore how Libby can continue to support you in your life's journey? Please see below.....

Love Yourself Sober - in this 8 module online course, Libby walks you through the exact process she designed herself, one day at a time, stepping into sobriety, to help you Love Yourself Sober too.

Step Into Your Soul Work - in this 8 week online course, Libby takes you through her Release-Align-Ascend method to heal limiting beliefs and abundance blocks, discover your soul's gifts and purpose and monetize your life's mission.

Become a Healer - SOSHA's apprenticeship program 'The Initiation' assists you to become a certified transformational healer, trained in self-healing techniques, using applied psychology, breathwork, Shamanism and quantum channeling to support yourself and others in their healing journeys.

Or find out more ways Libby may be able to help you and your business enterprise to create more success, in true alignment with your soul.....by heading to.....

www.libbyrobertson.com

@libbylightleader

hello@libbyrobertson.com

ABOUT THE PUBLISHER

Have It All Publishing is a newly established publishing house created with you, the author, in mind.

We know that true leaders wish to lead by example, which is why having a high-quality book and launch strategy is of the upmost importance.

But let's be honest—the traditional route is time-consuming, expensive, and fraught with ownership issues, while self-publishing is a minefield of uncertainty.

The solution?

Have It All Publishing!

We guide you through every step of the publishing process, including manuscript evaluation, editing, design, marketing, and more.

We believe in you and your story, and we're committed to keeping costs down and quality high so that you can share your message with the world.